YOU MUST BECOME AN ALGORITHMIC PROBLEM

Renegotiating the
Socio-Technical Contract

José Marichal

First published in Great Britain in 2025 by

Bristol University Press
University of Bristol
1–9 Old Park Hill
Bristol
BS2 8BB
UK
t: +44 (0)117 374 6645
e: bup-info@bristol.ac.uk

Details of international sales and distribution partners are available at bristoluniversitypress.co.uk

© Bristol University Press 2025

British Library Cataloguing in Publication Data
A catalogue record for this book is available from the British Library

ISBN 978-1-5292-4471-7 hardcover
ISBN 978-1-5292-4472-4 paperback
ISBN 978-1-5292-4473-1 ePub
ISBN 978-1-5292-4474-8 ePdf

The right of José Marichal to be identified as author of this work has been asserted by him in accordance with the Copyright, Designs and Patents Act 1988.

All rights reserved: no part of this publication may be reproduced, stored in a retrieval system, or transmitted in any form or by any means, electronic, mechanical, photocopying, recording, or otherwise without the prior permission of Bristol University Press.

Every reasonable effort has been made to obtain permission to reproduce copyrighted material. If, however, anyone knows of an oversight, please contact the publisher.

The statements and opinions contained within this publication are solely those of the author and not of the University of Bristol or Bristol University Press. The University of Bristol and Bristol University Press disclaim responsibility for any injury to persons or property resulting from any material published in this publication.

Bristol University Press works to counter discrimination on grounds of gender, race, disability, age and sexuality.

Cover design: Liam Roberts Design
Front cover image: Stocksy/Yaroslav Danylchenko

Contents

Introduction: You Must Become an Algorithmic Problem		1
1	How Much of a Problem Are We?	11
2	The Politics of Optimization	24
3	The Problem for Democracy	34
4	The Algorithmic Contract and its Discontents	43
5	The Classification Economy	66
6	Optimizing Identity	85
7	Algorithmic Obligation	105
References		123
Index		139

Introduction: You Must Become an Algorithmic Problem

In Phillip K. Dick's 1968 novel *Do Androids Dream of Electric Sheep?*, the author introduces the concept of kipple. The main character, Deckard, describes kipple as 'useless objects, like junk mail or match folders after you use the last match … if you go to bed leaving any kipple around your apartment, when you wake up the next morning there's twice as much of it' (Dick 1996, 65). The novel, the basis of which became the iconic dystopian 1982 movie *Blade Runner*, presents a post-nuclear world in which the line between real and artificial is blurred by human-like androids.

We wage a daily fight against kipple in our current technologically saturated age. We are bombarded with digital information from a hoard of devices: our laptops, our phones, our Ring cameras, our Alexas, our Kindles, and so on. The stream of information is so overwhelming that it often seems as if we are powerless to know what information is useful and which is not. Kipple was meant by Dick to represent the futility of fighting against 'entropy' – the descent into disorder and chaos. In the novel, Dick suggests that the fight against kipple is futile – 'no one can win' against its relentless expansion (Dick 1996, 65).

How do we fight against *informational kipple*? In this book, I make the claim that we navigate the information overwhelm through an *algorithmic contract*. It is an arrangement we may not be aware we are entering. In this contract, we entrust tech companies and powerful elites to help us manage this information flood by allowing ourselves to be optimized and classified through recommendation algorithms. Trusting these classifications helps us make sense of the information flood and lessens our anxieties about an increasingly complex world. In exchange, we allow ourselves to be 'made more predictable' by behaving more and more in accordance to how the algorithm classifies us. Through the deployment of data capture devices and analytical calculations, algorithms 'optimize' us to become predictable through the amplification of our preferences, subtly sorting us into like-minded clusters. This steering allows us to perform more predictably as consumer subjects and also as citizens.

What happens to our interest in, or capacity to defend, liberal democracy when each of us are encouraged by subtle forces to 'fit the predictive model'? The practice of model fitting in supervised machine learning demands the accumulation of more and more training data to 'reduce the cost function' and to improve 'model fit'. Those who are not accurately predicted by the model are problematic 'outliers'. If you 'curve the line' to accommodate outliers in your training data, then you run the risk of 'overfitting' the training or cross-validation data, hence making it not as useful for prediction. But, if you ignore the outlier, you will misclassify cases, and your model will be sub-optimal.

The outlier serves as a useful metaphor for our changing role in larger society. Should we as citizens of liberal democracies remain problematic outliers, defying categorization and optimization? With a few exceptions, we fail to connect this core data science problem to the broader sociopolitical context in which we formulate our political attitudes. The ways in which algorithmic models classify subjects into patterns or clusters have radical implications for how we see ourselves, each other, and our political institutions. What does it mean to live in a society where more of our fellow citizens strive to 'fit the model'?

In this book, I explore this idea of an outlier and the ways in which we, in our online and physical environments, are losing a sense of individuality and idiosyncrasy. I examine why we need to be outliers in liberal democracy, arguing that outliers provide the epistemological capacity to offer innovative solutions to vexing challenges. Increasingly, being anachronistic in a world increasingly impacted by algorithmic optimization can make one feel overwhelmed by the kipple. But citizens who remain algorithmic problems are critical to liberal democracies.

The algorithmic contract

This evolving landscape of data collection, algorithmic prediction, and personalized targeting raises profound questions about privacy, autonomy, and human agency. In our increasingly digital world, algorithmic models take every typed word or gesture (likes), eye movement, or swipe and breaks them down into either a node (thing) or an edge (attribute), which is placed into a database. This age of incessant collecting and analysing of our digital life is what I call an *algorithmic age*. In the algorithmic age, the priority is to create products that can predict our future behaviour. Prior to the 2010s, prediction was important, but understanding ourselves and other humans was the priority. We have moved into a regime where data is collected not simply to understand humans for marketing or surveillance purposes, but to create artificial replicas of human thought.

Research and lived experiences increasingly show that most people are not 'battling against the kipple'. They are content to accept a world of algorithmic classification despite its obvious harms because it gives them a (false) promise of comfort and security. We continue to be glued to our devices, increasingly using social media platforms as the foundation of our information diets. A 2024 Pew study found that 86 per cent of users got their news from digital devices, and a growing number (54 per cent) sometimes or often get their news from social media platforms. On social media sites popular with young people, 40 per cent of Instagram users and 52 per cent of TikTok users regularly get their news from each platform (St. Aubin and Liedke 2024a). If we are under the throes of algorithmic overlords, we are not acting like it.

For this reason, we should think of our relationship to algorithms through the lens of contract theory. The concept of a social contract is a core element of political theory. Political theorists have used it to justify why individuals should form allegiances to a particular political system. It is a thought experiment designed to illustrate a relationship, one that cannot possibly be universal in practice since individuals have different reasons for their allegiance to a state. Nonetheless, it is one that provides legitimacy for state power. The three most prominent applications of contract theory come from Locke, Rousseau, and Hobbes, who posit that rational actors will willingly give up their theoretical position in a 'state of nature' either for protection of the self (Hobbes 1967 [1651]) or for an increased preservation of rights (Locke 1996). In Rousseau's (1920 [1762]) case, leaving the state of nature is a fact and the only way to restore a sense of meaning and an escape from the judgement and status consciousness of modernity is to submit to your political community – the general will. In each case, the social contract justifies adherence to a political system. The system will either protect your physical person (Hobbes 1967 [1651]), preserve your natural rights (Locke 1996 [1689]), or provide you with meaning (Rousseau 1920 [1762]).

The contract perspective is a useful framework for understanding our relationship with engagement algorithms. The Internet presents us with a vast, unlimited field of information and cultural content. This expansiveness is prone to making us anxious. To relieve our anxiety, we cede our curational autonomy to the algorithm. By allowing the algorithm to curate our information/cultural environments, we get relief from the 'anxiety of choice'. In exchange for a condition of curated information abundance and expanded access to the tools of voice, we allow platforms and other companies to extract our data and use it in this process of algorithmic curation. Through this data extraction, algorithms more narrowly curate our information environments and group us into consumer clusters for marketing purposes. These 'new identities' we formulate through the algorithm promise to make sense of a complex, contingent world by narrowing the scope and making it appear more certain. By eliminating content that we find dissonant or uncomfortable or packaging the content in ways that allow us to mock or shame dissonant content, we get an information/cultural environment which feels more cognitively comfortable and less anxiety provoking. In addition, we get tools like Ring cameras, which can give us the illusion of safety by making us dependent on 'personal anomaly detectors' which scan our environment for 'threatening' anomalies.

As with the Lockean and Hobbesian contracts, no one 'signs' a contract, but the thought experiment provides a way of understanding the relationship between the subject and the state. Similarly, the algorithmic contract is an effort to theorize our acquiescence to algorithmic governance in this new age. This contract comes with unintended consequences. The Internet was sold to us as a revolutionary platform that would break down barriers to knowledge, communication, and self-expression. Early blogging platforms and Internet culture produced a brilliant explosion of creative output. The web of the early 2010s was heralded as the vehicle to express democracy and freedom in the face of tyranny and oppression. If anything, social media liberates rather than inhibits, so the thought went. But this ability to express ourselves came with a predicament. Our desire to 'be heard' and to express ourselves is an indelible fact of our humanity – the desire to search for our authentic self is the same thing that compels us to produce data. But to express ourselves in an attention economy requires that we modify our voice if we want to 'be heard'. This changes expression from something that emerges from a fixed self that seeks to *express*, to a malleable identity that adjusts oneself to *be heard*.

In the last decade, the rapid acceleration of wireless data transmission capacity, the capacity for data storage, and increased processor speeds have produced an analysis revolution. Entire fields of business intelligence, cybersecurity, and so on have grown exponentially in the last decade. By the mid-2010s it was starting to become obvious that the vast trough of user posts generated by hundreds of millions of social media users could be beneficial as marketing intelligence. The monetization insight was that human expression could be tokenized and placed into models that add predictive value to marketers. This puts individual opinion into the world of supply and demand. If opinion is a commodity, then a lack of it poses a problem. If users are not on their devices enough, then there is a supply challenge. To remedy this, the priority for platforms is to make the production of opinion and engagement habitual.

At that point, encouraging users to stay on the platform to render opinions/produce content generates more material that can be 'datafied' and used for machine learning prediction and AI (artificial intelligence) training. The effect of the commodification of Internet engagement was that the market incentives became driven by emphasizing 'being heard' (voice) at the expense of expressing oneself (thought). Self-expression requires reflection to know what one wants or needs to say. Speaking (voice) does not require thought.

Voice can be immediate, instinctive, and reactionary, generated through simple appeals to affect and desire. Reflection is not as easy to monetize.

An abundance of the expression of voice seems like an endless resource. If we had listening devices attached to us all day, the well of expression would not run dry. While studies vary, the average person in Western societies speak about 16,000 words a day (Mehl et al 2007). If the market incentives are to extract voice from us, it does not really matter with whom we are talking. A recent estimate from a former United States intelligence official estimates that upwards of 80 per cent of accounts on X (formerly Twitter) were bot accounts (Woods 2022).

The outlier problem in machine learning

The role of a quantitative social science that uses statistical modelling is to close the gap between the reality being studied and the abstraction of the model. In graduate school, I was trained to believe that there was a distinction between the world as it is and our need to abstract it or to make sense of it. If an econometric model abstracts too much (has too few variables/parameters), the resulting model might be overly simplistic, missing the subtleties in the broader population it seeks to understand. On the other hand, if the model is not abstract enough (has too many parameters), the model may become excessively complex, making it challenging to understand the underlying dynamics, thereby violating the law that models should be parsimonious to maximize explanatory power. Simple models that explain a great deal are considered to be 'elegant' (that is, they explain a lot with few variables). There is humility to this approach. It recognizes that models are abstractions of the real. This was a necessity because in the world before machine learning and AI, we did not have endless resources to collect data on entire populations of individuals. Samples carefully selected allowed us to infer from models we create about a population at large. It is impossible to explain any phenomena fully because there are always cases that violate expectations. In statistics, we call these outliers: confounding cases not explained by the model in its current state. Advances in science come from adding explanatory variables (understanding) to a model that can increase its power. Additionally, throwing too many variables into a model can produce a 'degrees of freedom' problem, where you have more variables than cases.

The data science/AI revolution has challenged that perceived limitation. There exists a push to blur the distinction between the world as it is and the world of the algorithm. Tech companies hire data engineers to push the limits of model optimization. How can we improve 'model fit'? Data scientists can push the boundaries of 'unknowability' by increasing the number of parameters/variables in the model or adding layers in a neural network. Parsimony is not a core concern in machine learning. With massive computational power, you can have billions of cases and hence billions of parameters. The space between model abstraction and reality narrows. The need to develop theory is lessened since explanation is not the point. The point is prediction.

Humans, however, are slippery subjects. A model that might explain behaviour at one point or in one context may not be as effective in another. The truth of human contingency makes prediction challenging. Humans are creatures of habit and pattern, but we also reflect on our habits and patterns and change them with changing circumstances. What makes us 'tick' is immanently complex and difficult to understand. The neuroscientist Jeff Lichtman describes the intricacies of how the brain works:

> If you can't understand New York City, it's not because you can't get access to the data. It's just that there's so much going on at the same time. That's what the human brain is. It's millions of things happening simultaneously among different types of cells, neuromodulators, genetic components, things from the outside. There's no point when you can suddenly say, 'I now understand the brain,' just as you wouldn't say, 'I now get New York City.' (Lichtman in Guitchounts 2021)

Much of modern machine learning is modelled upon the workings of the human brain (neural networks). In a neural network, each layer comprises a set of attributes (features) and each neuron in the network is given a particular weight based on the predictive importance of the feature. There are endless ways by which we can be classified. We can be broken down into tens of thousands of attributes (eye colour, hair colour or waist circumferences as examples), and ranked or clustered on them based on the objective. This constellation of features and weights is what makes us distinctive, but, in a neural network, we are broken down into component parts. The task is to determine which of our features improves prediction or classification. One popular machine learning algorithm, 'gradient descent', adjusts the 'weights' for the different parameters in the model until the model arrives at a 'local minima' that optimizes the model's predictive value (reduces the cost function).

The magic of neural networks is that the allocation of weights is not driven by theory. Through 'backpropagation', the model moves back through the layers of the neural network, adjusting the magnitude and direction of weights to produce the 'right answer' after it has compared one training case to the output in the final layer. If the output of a particular case looks like 'random noise' or does poorly at prediction (that is, has a high cost function) then it will 'propagate back' to the previous layer adjusting the direction in the magnitude of the weights to minimize the cost function (that is, *get closer to the right answer*).

This is what I refer to in this book as the *algorithmic problem*. To be an outlier, not behaving in ways that are predictable to the algorithm, impacts 'model fit'. In the language of machine learning, a 'difficult to classify' case is one that makes it more challenging to 'reduce the cost function' of the model (that is, improve the 'fit' of the model in predicting the data). We know little about what it means for us to be broken down into a set of potentially thousands of features that are weighted to give whoever is conducting the analysis powerful clues as to how any one of us behaves. If the models are limited in their effectiveness, one of two things is possible: a) there is not enough data to accurately predict, or b) we are too variable and unpredictable to ever become a problem that can be solved algorithmically. If 'a' is the case, the solution is to collect more data. If 'b' is closer to reality, what is the answer? With limitations as to the extent to which data and algorithms can predict us, the answer to the optimization problem would require changing the behaviour of the subject so they behave in ways that are more consistent with the model. Put into the language of machine learning: there is an increasing danger that instead of algorithms predicting us better, we are encouraged to behave in accordance with the algorithmic recommendation. We develop what Airoldi (2021) calls a 'machine habitus', sorting and classifying the world around us in ways that move us towards our algorithmically determined self. The model classifies us, but we also learn to 'classify ourselves', or, in the language of gradient descent, we 'move towards the local minima'.

Outline of the book

In the pages that follow, I will explore the effects of the algorithmic contract on liberal democracy and how we are incentivized to 'optimize towards our classification'. I will discuss the role that the algorithmic contract plays in de-emphasizing outliers – those idiosyncratic individuals who add value to democratic life through providing alternative viewpoints and retaining independent thought. The challenge in our algorithmically mediated society is for each of us to 'remain an algorithmic problem', supported by social values, norms, and institutions that prioritize cultivating a need for human creativity and spontaneity. Serendipity, I will argue, is a valuable tool for cultivating personal and democratic health, along with a keen ability to be engaged in the life of one's community. We need to develop and have opportunities to utilize skills of human discernment.

This book starts with questioning whether human behaviour is a solvable algorithmic problem. In Chapter 1, I explore the consequences of the algorithmic contract on human autonomy. I argue that we trade our autonomy for algorithmic curation, voice, and the security of curation and classification. I explore how data brokers, tech companies, and government agencies support this contract, engaging in a 'digital gold rush' to make human behaviour predictable and knowable through data collection and analysis. I discuss the nature of the outlier problem in machine learning and emphasize the impact of locating the local minima in a stepwise fashion. I use this as a metaphor for how algorithms steer us towards optimizing their classification of us. This algorithmic mediation is threatening liberal democracy by reducing humans to classified subjects and treating outliers as an algorithmic problem rather than valuable sources of creativity and social progress.

In Chapter 2, I discuss the cultural consequences of a *politics of optimization*. The increased sophistication of algorithmic optimization is not only altering how individuals view themselves as political and social agents, but is changing culture (music, art, gaming, architecture) by homogenizing design to conform to the dictates of the algorithm. I discuss how the optimization mandate embeds a politics that perpetuates biases and reinforces existing social and political norms. I discuss how optimization leads to a culture of sameness and stagnation in various fields, including music, art, and architecture. This is largely driven by creators adjusting their creative expression to optimize for the algorithms. This leads to a homogenization of cultural production, a lack of innovation, and a reinforcement of existing power structures.

In Chapter 3, I discuss what different 'optimization regimes' would mean for citizenship. I look at different approaches for optimization of algorithmic citizens, promoting a 'virtuous citizen' that emphasizes human telos and state promotion of virtuous behaviour through algorithmic management. I also look at a 'preservation of the self' approach that prioritizes algorithmic surveillance to ensure physical safety through predictive policing, social media monitoring, and facial recognition, and conclude by examining a 'preservation of rights' approach that promotes individual autonomy and choice. I argue that a preservation of rights view serves as a foundation for what the algorithmic contract promises because it presumes the user as an autonomous choosing agent. Rather than seeing the vast amount of choice the Internet provides as freedom, I use the work of Eran Fisher (2022) to argue that the unlimited choice present in our online lives is a source of anxiety. In Chapter 4, I discuss how the algorithmic contract promises to relieve anxiety by removing the *burden of choosing* through recommendation algorithms and subsequent classification. A consequence of the algorithmic contract is the creation of an 'ordinal society' (Fourcade and Healy 2024), where our online lives are used to continuously categorize and sort us algorithmically. I discuss how this ordinal society produces a shift in our identities once rooted in place or in ascribed characteristics. The algorithmic contract paradoxically offers agency, while accelerating 'ordinalization'. It conflates choice with anxiety reduction and risk management. Through algorithms that curate our information and entertainment environments, the algorithmic contract is disguised as empowerment: aiding our transformation into simpler, 'better' versions of ourselves. However, this empowerment comes with a shift in our relationship with the natural world, as every technological advance increases abstraction and detachment from it. This illusion of control and empowerment comes at a steep cost because we are implicitly encouraged to 'move towards the local minima' in a fashion similar to what happens in gradient descent models that seek to 'reduce the cost function'.

In Chapter 5, I explore the neoliberal basis of the algorithmic contract. I discuss the assumptions of classical Austrian economists about how markets operate, emphasizing market efficiency, individual priority, and a minimal state. Algorithmic optimization challenges assumptions about the information environment between buyers and sellers and the independence of preference formation. Platforms like Uber and Amazon use algorithms to personalize prices and curate choices. This algorithmic contract presents users as isolated, atomized agents but, in reality, algorithms steer choice towards the local minima of classification. I use Matthew Flisfeder's (2021) *Algorithmic Desire: Toward a New Structuralist Theory of Social Media* to highlight how algorithms create desire by producing a continuous condition of lack, making us anxious and longing. Because algorithms cannot satisfy our desires, our impulses get expressed in perverse, anti-social ways that breed isolation and commodification. I connect this to Adam Fish's (2017) 'technoliberalism' which argues that technology promises to use neoliberal solutions to solve progressive social problems. I detail critiques of this approach, highlighting that the 'optimization mandate' of technoliberalism produces a shift from *convivial tools* to *tools of suspicion* by selling risk reduction technologies that amplify a sense of danger and paranoia. I argue that the optimization and classification the algorithmic contract provides has the effect of narrowing our worldviews, which in turn amplifies our suspicion. I then turn to luxury surveillance tools, like Ring cameras, which reinforce this anxiety and turn users into citizen anomaly detectors.

In Chapter 6, I discuss why the algorithmic contract has such an allure in the United States. I draw upon the American romantics (Whitman, Emerson, Thoreau) to discuss the ways in which the algorithmic contract appeals to users' sense of their unique 'inner spark'. This prioritization of the individual and their unique experience resonates in the algorithmic contract, which falsely promises to foster self-discovery. In fact, it undermines users' search for their authentic selves by prioritizing the security/risk mitigation over innovation. I extend this thinking to the heroic status we give Silicon Valley technologists, likening their discoveries to the myth of American manifest destiny. I explore how this heroic status gives tech entrepreneurs license to treat everything as a 'frontier' (Turner 2013). This includes using behavioural science techniques to manipulate user behaviour. Using Beer's

(2022) observation that the algorithmic contract promises a 'new life' that lures users into a simplified, abstracted identity, I discuss the social harms this creates: from amplifying engagement with commercial 'non-things' (Han 2022) to encouraging collective conformity, amplifying indignation, conspiracy, and a cynicism that fuels reactionary politics. I conclude by likening our submission to algorithmic prediction to the practice of industrial factory farming in the United States and the environmental, public health, and ethical externalities that result from an optimization framework.

I conclude in Chapter 7 by exploring what we can do to *remain algorithmic problems*. I build upon Risse's (2023) focus on epistemic rights, which includes protecting individuals as knowers and knowns. I argue that algorithms also have obligations to promote democratic pluralism, diverse narratives, and a 'right to be epistemologically challenged'. Users should expect that algorithms contribute to their fostering of a meaningful digital life, respecting the complexity and depth of human experience, and promoting play, creativity, and encounter. I present three principles that are central to an expanded algorithmic obligation: an emphasis on serendipity, a right to synthetic potentiality, and a fostering of Boolean fuzziness. Each of these principles focus on cultivating a sense of epistemological capacity. I argue that these things will only happen if users demand a renegotiation of the algorithmic contract, which currently gives an asymmetrical advantage to tech elites. I argue that we are in what Kalyvas (2008) called an 'extraordinary moment' in our technological life for legitimacy and change. I conclude by discussing Bonini and Trere's (2024) *Algorithms of Resistance: The Everyday Fight against Platform Power*, which highlights users' everyday resistance against algorithmic domination. I argue that everyday resistance must build towards mobilizing for systemic change. A renegotiation requires users to reject platforms that classify them, encouraging 'exit' to algorithm-free alternatives like pi.fyi or 'dumb phones'. This 'exit' is a starting point for users reclaiming their agency and compelling tech firms to renegotiate the terms of the algorithmic contract in ways that maintain human autonomy and 'the outlier'.

1

How Much of a Problem Are We?

In 2017, the Cambridge Analytica scandal looked like something out of a Hollywood movie. Even the president of the organization, Alexander Nix, sounded and looked faintly like a Bond villain. Cambridge Analytica, a 'global election management agency', created 'psychographic' profiles on individual voters based on the harvesting of millions of Facebook accounts, which allegedly allowed it to create targeted online content based on individual personality profiles. Aleksandr Kogan, a Cambridge University researcher, built a Facebook app called 'thisisyourdigitallife' under the premise of collecting academic research. The app would invite users to take a personality test. A small number of users (about 270,000) originally installed the app. Upon installation, the app asked users to give it permission to access their Facebook profile (which included information regarding their Facebook friends). Kogan was able to use a loophole in Facebook's terms of service allowing academics to access its data interface (API, or application programming interface) for research. Kogan was then able to gain access to data on fifty million users, not just the 270,000 that had installed the app.

The data was used to create profiles constructed from the Big Five/OCEAN personality dimensions (openness, conscientiousness, extroversion, agreeableness, and neuroticism). In dozens of news stories, documentaries, and presentations, Cambridge Analytica would make outlandish claims about their ability to create effective ads 'micro-targeted' to an individual's psychometric profile. For example, users whose profiles were more conscientious (hence prone to seeing external threats in the environment) would get ads targeted to evoke an anxiety response. After Donald Trump's surprise victory in the 2016 US election, befuddled political observers seeking ready answers to how he could have won latched on to Cambridge Analytica as a core explanation. Although it is unclear whether the data was influential in Trump's eventual victory, the incident highlighted flaws in how social media companies protect user data. The case was a pivotal moment, leading to a series of investigations, hearings, and changes in policies regarding third-party access to user data.

In 2017, the possibility that this emerging field of micro-targeting could 'predict subjects' was both terrifying and mesmerizing. Psychometric profiling has a mystique that makes it appear powerful. Even the US Central Intelligence Agency engaged in psychometric profiling operations (Lantz 1987). Despite the ominous nature of Cambridge Analytica's practices, this outfit was also overpromising. For years in my Internet and Politics class, I used a website called *Apply Magic Sauce* that could create a psychometric profile based on a user's social media posts. The site would 'magically' produce robust insights into an individual's personality based on their likes, shares, and status updates. But every time I used this site with my students, it produced less than impressive results.

A more important question than whether Cambridge Analytica was effective in predicting behaviour is why Cambridge Analytica existed in the first place. We do not have to take a class in finance or marketing to know that companies are desperate for data that can accurately 'predict' consumers, especially as it pertains to consumer behaviour. By now, we are aware of (if not comfortable) with the idea that our online data is collected, analysed, and packaged to companies seeking to market products to us. The scope of this practice, however, continues to be poorly understood by users.

As Byron Tau (2024) points out in his book, *Means of Control: How the Hidden Alliance of Tech and Government Is Creating a New American Surveillance State*, the data broker industry is growing at a breathtaking pace. Brokers are in a mad dash to produce the next technology that will facilitate mass data collection. Tau analogizes this to prospectors in a digital gold rush. As he notes, it is not simply companies that want this data; increasingly, state/local and federal government agencies are clients. This is true despite the fact that the empirical research on the effectiveness of psychometric profiling on campaigns remains scant. While some studies find that one's digital footprint is predictive of Big Five personality traits (Azucar et al 2018), there is little work that ties these traits to political behaviour. Appel and Matz (2021) found that psychological profiling could increase ad engagement but likely had little effect on persuasion. Eady et al (2023) found that the Russian government's psychometric profiling campaigns had little to no effect on the 2016 election. Sumpter (2018) evaluated the Big Five/OCEAN model on a smaller sample of Facebook users and found that the model only predicted the absence or presence of a trait 60 per cent of the time for four of the traits (conscientiousness, extroversion, agreeableness, and neuroticism) and 65 per cent of the time for openness. This is only slightly better than random chance (50 per cent). However, Laterza (2021) argues that psychographic profiling is part of a broader, more effective, digital ethnographic profiling of voters.

It is difficult to disentangle the reality of Cambridge Analytica from the hype. Whether or not, it is possible for an organization to 'know us' from a collection of Facebook posts or if Cambridge Analytica was effective, the incentives to make us 'knowable' are pervasive. The market for 'algorithmic knowing' packages users as commodities to interested parties (advertisers, law enforcement, corporations, and so on). These 'biopolitical companies' (Herder 2019), a reference to Foucault's concept of biopower, describes companies who profit by supplying nation states and other entities with the data analytic tools needed to regulate and control populations (Foucault 1976). These companies comprise a vast network of platforms, data brokers, health data firms, security and analytics firms, and others that gather, and analyse data for the purpose of predicting human and social behaviour. These firms have a wide range of vendors that include state agencies like intelligence agencies and law enforcement.

The fact that a 'social media panic' ensued after the 2016 election was not seen negatively by the large tech platforms (even though Facebook had to pay a fine to the Federal Trade Commission). A social media panic is in the interest of companies like Facebook that benefit from outlandish claims regarding how much companies can 'predict' users (Vinsel 2021). Social media platforms and the data-driven marketing industry in general benefit from the idea that they have more predictive capabilities from their users' data than is empirically provable (Zuboff 2019). This fear is far from unfounded. In 2016, Russia's Internet Research Agency (IRA) hired people to create fake accounts that looked like they belonged to Americans with the sole purpose of causing discord by pushing inflammatory material. While, by one estimate, 126 million people saw IRA-related posts, the impact it had on the 2016 election was hard to discern (Isaac and Wakabayashi 2017).

Even if Cambridge Analytica was hype, there remains a deep desire among a network of actors (tech companies, data brokers, marketers, political campaigns, and governments) to realize *the promise* of Cambridge Analytica. Cambridge Analytica is not significantly different from any other company engaged in data collection and/or analysis. This type of company depends upon a certain hype that helps cement their image as techno-mystical, selling algorithms as a miraculous tool that unpacks and lays bare human behaviour.

While there are serious long-term concerns about the accelerated development of AI, an esoteric argument about rogue superintelligence misses a more pressing challenge: to what extent can these emerging technologies predict our behaviour? Is the secret to predicting humanity a matter of data availability and storage capacity? Will AI overcome the seeming contingency and unpredictability of human existence via quantum computing, advances in algorithmic optimization, increased data collection, and improved storage? If so, an algorithm that can truly 'know' humans would rob us of our human and political agency. The ability of AI algorithms to 'know' us might be limited now, but algorithms are getting better at this task.

Are outliers an engineering problem?

Universal to all humans is subjectivity – an ability to reflect on our experience. The enlightenment liberal idea is that humans, reflecting autonomous selves, should pursue their view of good. Immanuel Kant's 'kingdom of ends' proposes that humans are ends in themselves and should have the ability to reflect on their condition or group membership and change it if they should (Kant 2017). Algorithms frustrate the principle of liberal autonomy in that they interfere with our ends by predicting and anticipating our desires, possibly before we even know them ourselves.

If prediction algorithms are able to *know us*, it would mean that we are an *engineering problem*. A proponent of this view would argue that predicting human behaviour is within the realm of the 'knowable' – subject only to having enough data, a storage capacity, and enough GPU (graphics processing unit) power to run the model. Even in the case of the 'idiosyncratic outlier', their behaviour might be a more vexing, yet achievable problem.

As evidence of the problem-solving capabilities of AI, Google's AlphaFold project, an AI developed by DeepMind, predicted all possible three-dimensional structures of proteins based on their amino acid sequences. This problem, called 'protein folding', is one of the great challenges in genetics research. The algorithm was able to predict the folding structure of all known proteins, unlocking potential sources of diseases and turbo-charging scientific discovery. This breakthrough saved hundreds of years of research time. Other AI models have made similar advances in materials science, cancer detection, and antibiotic discovery. These discoveries prompted Dario Amodei (2024), one of the co-founders of Anthropic, to predict 'the defeat of most diseases, the growth in biological and cognitive freedom, the lifting of billions of people out of poverty to share in the new technologies, [and] a renaissance of liberal democracy and human rights' in the next 5 to 10 years. Could we have similar discoveries in the social sciences? The process of computationally aided prediction of human behaviour is fraught with ethical and metaphysical questions. Deism, the belief that God created the world and allowed it to operate according to natural laws, links science to faith. This is represented in a 'watchmaker' notion of God, as embraced by the 18th-century Freemasons, and rooted in the belief that scientific discovery uncovers God's truths. A deist might argue that God is at the end of the 'human engineering puzzle' of making us *knowable* through algorithms.

Max Weber (1946) believed that replacing a religious understanding of the world with a scientific one created a 'disenchantment' in modernity. Instead of seeing the world as magical and divinely inspired, we use scientific language to explain transcendent, divine phenomena. The rise of AI and algorithmic systems presents a paradoxical development: while founded on scientific rationalism, these technologies introduce elements of enchantment and mysticism back into contemporary life. Transformer models and neural networks with billions of parameters are too complex for scientists to be able to explain how models arrive at the generated output. The opacity and inscrutability of AI decision-making processes imbue these systems with a quasi-mystical quality. The 'black box' nature of machine learning algorithms creates an aura of mystery around AI capabilities and outputs (Pasquale 2015). Additionally, recommendation algorithms curate personalized digital experiences in ways that can feel revelatory, like a form of *magic*.

At first glance, algorithms and AI serve as the basis for re-enchanting the world. Deep learning algorithms, such as the one behind AlphaGo, can process vast amounts of data at breakneck speed with models patterned after the human brain. Neural networks contain layers of neurons that represent different values. These neurons are arranged in layers that represent different attributes that aid prediction or generation. The algorithm learns how to adjust the weights of each parameter to arrive at the 'right answer' in a prediction algorithm. Other algorithms like adversarial networks have a slightly different architecture. The complexity inherent in the process (the number of parameters and the depth of layers) makes it nearly impossible to understand how the neural net arrives at an answer. This powerful technology has revolutionized approaches to cancer detection and financial fraud. Technological complexity, however, scrambles the basis of the enlightenment project by prioritizing prediction over understanding. When we lose the scientific language to understand the world, then we are left trying to make sense of AI predictions.

If you knew nothing about natural language processing, you would likely have a sense of enchantment over the questions 'how does Siri know what I want?' and 'how does Alexa know when I say "I want to play rock" that I am asking for music and not to literally play with a rock?' Algorithms turn everything we say into structured data, but most of us are not sure how (including some AI designers). While still in its infancy, the gains in abstract reasoning ability have led some in the AI community to be concerned about an 'alignment problem' – 'super-intelligent' or 'rogue' AI who might act in ways not aligned with humanity's values or interests.

The existential threat to humanity via the so-called 'alignment problem' reinforces the status of AI as an overwhelmingly powerful entity: so powerful that, if you are a company, you best invest a significant number of resources to stay competitive. This mindset does not only apply to companies, but to people. To compete in the economy of the future, you should know how to work with AI. The enchantment of AI creates a Cold War tech race between companies and individuals to bolster their AI skills to remain competitive. In 2023, 191,000 tech workers were laid off in the United States (Crunchbase 2024). In June of 2024, the financial firm JP Morgan announced that it was going to require every new hire to get prompt engineering training for AI (Levitt 2024).

This is by design. Companies like OpenAI, Alphabet, Anthropic, Meta, and others are following the same playbook: roll out generative AI products that create a sense of 'shock and awe' among the public. Even 'doomerism' about an AI apocalypse is part of the design. In late 2022 to early 2023, improvement in the latest generation of transformer-based, large language attention models, like OpenAI's ChatGPT 3, and image generator models, like Stable Diffusion, caught observers by surprise. At the time of writing in May 2025, improvements in the size, speed and computational efficiency of AI models were happening daily. This has observers worried about the ability of AI to manipulate users and influence elections. In a worst-case scenario, AI could be used to create weapons that destroy humanity.

For example, a team of Swiss researchers took MegaSyn, a machine learning model published by Collaborations Pharmaceuticals Inc., which was trained to identify potential pharmaceutical drugs, and asked it to come up with toxic compounds that would mirror the composition of VX nerve gas (Urbina 2022). In less than six hours, the algorithm identified 40,000 potential biological weapons. The researchers presented this work at an international security conference to raise awareness of the dangers of AI if misused. In pre-modern societies, this awesome power was reserved for God.

In his 2007 book, *A Secular Age*, Charles Taylor argued that the immanent (God in the world) and the secular (enlightenment rationality) exist in tension with one another in modern society. He rejected what he calls the 'subtraction narrative', (Taylor 2007, 27) where reason replaces religion and disenchants the world. Modernity signals a shift from an enchanted pre-modern world where phenomena were explained through magic to one where science creates doubt about the presence of the divine. This produces a 'buffered self' that does not allow itself to experience 'fullness' (Taylor 2007, 41). For Taylor, the pre-modern self was constantly cognizant of the spiritual realm and open to transcendent experiences. He calls this pre-modern self a 'porous self'. This world of doubt and uncertainty, where the scientific and the religious coexist, inhibits the development of a porous self that can experience moments of fullness. Magic and ritual served as a sincere effort to control frightening and awesome external forces (natural disasters, wars, diseases, and so on). By contrast, the modern self creates a barrier between the individual and this external spiritual world. This means that while religion is obviously still a major part of modernity, faith is separated from everyday life. In modernity, religion is one logic among many (capitalism, artistic, fame, and so on). Hence, for most, it is no longer the central organizing force of life (Taylor 2007).

Taylor's framework is useful for positing how we as subjects are responding to our *algorithmic age*. Are AI and algorithms re-enchanting us and encouraging us to be open to experiences of fullness? Or are we using the enchanted nature of algorithms and AI the way pre-moderns used religion: to control frightening and formidable external forces, but without the sense of fullness that many claim comes with religious faith? I posit that we are turning to algorithms to buffer us against the increasing complexity and perceived dangers of the outside world. As such, we are willingly becoming more disenchanted, buffered subjects who accept an algorithmically mediated reality that inhibits our individuality and autonomy in exchange for perceived certitude and perceived security. I refer to this trade throughout the book as an *algorithmic contract*, modelled on the social contracts of modern political thinkers like Hobbes and Locke. The algorithmic contract is such that we trade our autonomy for the promise of voice, curation, and classification. In terms of algorithmic computation, the outlier switches from being a wondrous, vexing subject that 'contains multitudes' to an 'anomaly' that the algorithm 'detects' to mitigate or eliminate.

By providing us with platforms where we can exercise voice, the algorithmic contract gives us the appearance of relevance, control, and agency. At the same time, engagement algorithms promise to relieve us from the anxiety of choosing (Fisher 2022) in an endless world of digital content. Platforms encourage us to produce opinions and content experiences, but algorithms encourage us to *classify ourselves* through our pursuit of interests by giving us more of what we previously asked for. This recursive loop of preference has the effect of narrowing our scope of consumption of information and entertainment. It also truncates and curates the digital 'world out there' in ways that make it more comprehensible to us and less anxiety provoking.

The social contract lens reveals possibilities for our relationships to algorithms. They do not promote transcendence or immanence or move us closer to Platonic ideals, the Aristotelian Golden Mean, Hegelian dialectics, Franz Fanon's 'end' of an oppressive colonial world, or any other imagined goal. If anything, the algorithmic contract re-enchants society by amplifying conspiracy theories, magical thinking, and extreme ideologies. AI-driven re-enchantment fails to reinstall a sense of wonder in the world. What algorithms offer to many is a shallow simulacrum of a distorted world that potentially sows the seeds of authoritarianism and detachment from the real. It provokes a nagging suspicion that humans are 'replaceable' abstractions, rendered somehow less valuable, less sacred if we can be classified and categorized. Those who choose to be 'idiosyncratic' and 'not fit' the model are not elevated as trailblazers, but instead are seen as inconveniences, or even as threats, to the social order. Allowing ourselves to be classified has serious implications for citizens' senses of themselves as social, economic, and political agents. The datafication of society is creating a society of abstracted, category-sorted selves.

Our social contract with algorithms forever changes how we see ourselves as political subjects. As more and more of our output is used to train large language models that are interoperable between mediums (such as text, words, images, video, motion, and so on), there is a tendency to think of ourselves less as political subjects acting in concert in public life, and more as datafied, classified, commodified selves, passively consuming and being consumed, akin to factory farmed animals, an idea I will return to in Chapter 4.

The power of data-driven advertising is likely to strengthen with the advent of AI. In April of 2023, OpenAI's Greg Brockman gave a TED Talk where he presented ChatGPT's ability to suggest a meal, draw an image of the meal, create a shopping list for the meal, and communicate with Instacart to place an order for the ingredients (Brockman 2023). This early demonstration of ChatGPT's ability highlighted the company's aim of positioning AI tools as 'assistants' that 'build a relationship' with users. In April of 2023, Snapchat introduced an AI feature with which users could engage (Kelly 2023). Chat AI as 'your personal assistant' or 'your friend' has the potential to exponentially increase the amount of data it collects about you (its ability to 'know' you).

The loss of individuals who resist classification has profound implications for liberal democracy. In the past, the outlier citizen was celebrated as one who has exemplary skill, produces scientific or commercial discoveries, or stands up for justice against tyranny and oppression. Malcolm Gladwell (2008) expanded on this notion in his book *Outliers*. His underlying assumption was that there was significant social, economic, and cultural value to cultivating these types of individuals. However, if we think of outliers from the perspective of machine learning algorithms, then they take on a distinctive character. They become a 'problem' for which the data scientist needs to account. I suggest that, aside from the statistical challenge outliers pose, there are strong social, economic, and political forces with incentives to reduce their presence and influence in society.

The outlier is often seen as dangerous because they challenge official orthodoxies. Labelled by those in power as non-conformists, they raise questions about traditional views. A society full of those who conform to norms would be predictable and, presumably, the social order would be more stable. It is no accident that non-conformists in our culture are often artists and inventors. By contrast, conformists are associated with order-preserving institutions (law enforcement, religious institutions, the military). John Lennon, upon learning of Elvis' death, proclaimed 'Elvis died the day he went into the army' in 1958. Presumably, Lennon meant that the conformist nature of the military removed any tendency towards rebelliousness, an ingredient necessary for innovation. But in our modern era, what are we rebelling against? The state? The church? The market?

Does the analogy still fit? The concern is not that algorithms classify, but who decides the goals of classification. The problem with the algorithmic contract is that we've replaced national and community identity with optimization. We have adopted a 'hustle culture' where our identity and sense of purpose comes from efficiency, productivity, and with a premium value on 'influencing' others. The presumption is that there is an optimal answer to all policy questions and the arrival at this answer is only a matter of applying computational logic.

'Knowability' and the state

In *Seeing Like a State*, James Scott (1998, 4) claims that nation states, for much of the 20th century, were in an era of 'high modernism' – seeking to build upon 'the rational design of social order commensurate with the scientific understanding of natural laws' to manage their populations. From Scott's perspective, to manage populations, they must become 'legible' (that is, have their preferences and behaviours understood). Legibility means being able to simplify, standardize, and quantify populations. The knowledge derived from this legibility would lead to more effective governance and was critical for core functions of the state – conscripting soldiers, collecting taxes, undertaking infrastructure projects, and, most importantly, preventing rebellions.

Often, efforts at legibility were crude or incomplete. Citizens kept their legibility hidden from the state. Remaining *illegible* was the tool the marginalized could use to resist state control. But legibility was challenging for the state for other reasons. Group cultural practices were too complex and idiosyncratic for states to easily understand them. Often, communities create second economies outside of the official economic channels. Other groups were nomadic, lacked written traditions, or had different conceptions of land use that frustrated the state's efforts to manage them. Any effort at legibility for Scott was an exercise in abstraction that would miss the 'local knowledge' (Scott 1998, 6) of the communities being 'made legible' and would thus lead to poor policy outcomes.

Technology has made legibility easier – maybe too easy. In *The Known Citizen: A History of Privacy in Modern America*, Igo (2020) echoes Scott's analysis. She argues that Americans have become increasingly known to the state, corporations, and other individuals through enhanced surveillance, data collection, and analysis. She notes a tension among Americans between wanting their privacy (to be unknown) and wanting to be recognized (to be seen). Technologies steadily evolved in the 20th century that exposed citizens to others (the postcard, the camera, the telephone). The smartphone, social media, the high-speed processor, and the engagement algorithm have turbocharged this dynamic.

Igo (2020) discusses a jurisprudential principle, put forth by Samuel Warren and Louis Brandeis (1890), of the 'inviolate personality'. The principle was that people deserved protection beyond simply their physical safety or property protection. The invention of the camera, for example, raised profound questions about who owned an image and whether individuals had a right to be protected from the exposure of being photographed. Citizens had a right to privacy over their inner life, their thoughts, emotions, and personal expressions. The individual should control 'the extent to which [their] thoughts and emotions were to be exposed to others' (Warren and Brandeis 1890, 198 in Czubik 2016, 215). Warren and Brandeis went as far as to suggest that this principle extended to a person's 'peace of mind' and 'robustness of thought and delicacy of feeling' (Warren and Brandeis 1890, 193 in Czubik 2016, 215).

The advent of the data broker industry places the inviolable personality concept under threat. The digitalization of everyday life has exposed personal data and digital identity in ways that make us less secure. The toxic nature of social media challenges the notion of 'peace of mind' and psychological freedom implied by Warren and Brandeis. The discourse environment, encouraged by recommendation algorithms, has done damage to the 'robustness of thought and delicacy of feeling' (Warren and Brandeis 1890, 193 in Czubik 2016, 215) of individuals such that we are inured to having our privacy regularly violated.

Technology allows states to get closer to the legibility that Scott (1998) thought was nearly impossible. Farrell and Fourcade (2023) build on Scott's high modernism by introducing the idea of 'high-tech modernism'. They draw distinctions between bureaucratic and algorithmic efforts at legibility. Both are 'technologies of hierarchical classification and intervention' (Farrell and Fourcade 2023, 150) that serve as systems of control in diverse ways. Algorithm control, for Farrell and Fourcade (2023, 150), is less overt: '[U]nlike their paper-pushing predecessors in bureaucratic institutions, the humans of high-tech modernism disappear behind an algorithmic curtain. The workings of algorithms are much less visible, even though they penetrate deeper into the social fabric than the workings of bureaucracies.' Data scientists often refer to the 'three V's' of modern data collection and analysis – 'velocity' (processing speed), 'volume' (amount of data), and 'variety' (types of data being collected and processed) (Laney 2001). These high speed, high feedback mechanisms for classification are 'emergent and dynamic' systems that can adjust to the changing preferences and behaviours of subjects much faster than bureaucratic methods (Farrell and Fourcade 2023, 152).

These classification technologies are so sophisticated, we might discover that we do not need legibility at all. High-tech modernism goes beyond making subjects legible to channel and modify behaviour towards consumerist ends. Algorithms can do the work of making subjects not simply legible, but *editable* – they do not simply reveal preferences but drive them. Engagement algorithms have a unique ability to 'overwhelm the will' (LaPalme 2018) by presenting users with content that surreptitiously triggers their personalized emotional buttons. This poses a cyclical relationship between users drawn to certain content for reasons they cannot completely explain and producers who quickly learn that, for a cluster of the population, certain content is habit forming. This manifests in unusual and harmful ways. In 2022, *WIRED* ran a story on new mothers who became addicted to the content of children becoming sick or dying on social media (Knibbs 2022). The author coins the term 'emotional rubbernecking' to describe the ways in which she has become habituated towards certain content:

> Despite the visceral distress they provoke, these videos keep appearing on my screen for a reason: because I watch them. Raptly. I remember the names and conditions of these imperiled children, whether they are living with San Filippo syndrome or enduring chemotherapy, whether they have just died of myocarditis or SIDs. In my case, the algorithms know that if they serve me content about bad things happening to children, I'll watch it. And this emotional rubbernecking is not rare. Many of the sick-baby accounts I've seen have hundreds of thousands of followers, and tens of millions of views on their most heartrending posts. (Knibbs 2022)

The promise of social media platforms to increase access to diverse voices has not made individuals feel more empowered. With the age of AI, we might have more leisure time, but that leisure is filled with efforts to 'keep up' with a dizzying array of events and to 'be heard' on a global rather than local scale. Rather than seeking to simply know us, algorithms shape us by fostering within us a 'new algorithmic identity' (Cheney-Lippold 2011). Algorithms classify individuals into identity categories they might not initially self-identify with or be identified as by friends and associates; however, they may gradually adapt to the classification. Cheney-Lippold (2011) builds upon Foucault's (1978) notion of biopower, using the term 'soft biopower' to describe how code and algorithms are used to subtly steer individuals towards a goal. This is different from biopower, where the state is the main actor using the tools of bureaucracy to classify individuals. Cheney Lippold (2011) refers to 'soft biopolitics' to describe the ends to which this biopower is applied, where subjects are classified by algorithms but not in ways that are pre-determined by state actors.

Soft biopolitics constitutes a seismic shift in the nature of power and legibility. Algorithms fundamentally shape how individuals and populations are defined. Individuals are categorized, not through experience, argument, and discourse, but through data and statistical analysis (Cheney Lippold 2011). These new forms of grouping ourselves are 'cybernetic' (Ashby 1956) – they operate on the logic of feedback loops (negative and positive stimuli), rather than through subjective experience. The difference between the discursive and the cybernetic is that the former involves an inner dialogue on how one wants to adjust one's behaviour to the visible external world, while the other is more automatic and self-operating. As Cheney-Lippold (2011, 168) describes it, 'patterns of correlation can be found in technologies of algorithmic categorization, of recombining and unifying heterogeneous elements of data that have no inner necessity or coherence'.

The algorithm engages in a process of categorization without the consent or input from the categorized. Through social media recommendations, the algorithm forms a kind of 'algorithmic path dependence' towards a particular aesthetic and ideological worldview. This is different than the categorization we saw in democratic societies before the algorithmic age, when mass marketing and audience segmentation happened via external categories (race, gender, ethnicity, religion, and so on). With mass marketing, the user sees the marketing appeal, can reflect upon it, and either accept it or reject it. Cybernetic categorization is unique to the individual and based on the aggregation of online choices. Cheney-Lippold (2011, 169) uses Deleuze's (1992, 14) term 'dividuals' to explain how online 'fragments' (Cheney-Lippold 2011, 169), created by the arbitrary collection and analysis of online data, are aggregated to produce a digital subject. These 'dividuals' are detached from physical selves, placed into cybernetic categories that compete with traditional identity categories.

This high-tech modernism is more pernicious than Scott's (1998) high modernism. With old bureaucratic methods of legibility, there was a possibility of being misread or the possibility of the subject being able to challenge their categorization. Even if the state classified you, you could remain an autonomous self, regardless of the actions of a distant bureaucracy. The citizen still had the form of resistance that comes with 'remaining illegible'. Although the state has retained its ability to target and oppress, bureaucratic control allowed one to maintain a sense of internal autonomy despite repression.

Algorithmic categorization, as opposed to bureaucratic categorization, includes feedback mechanisms that cannot only alter the classifications, but can shape and modify the self so that it more squarely fits into the categorization. Farrell and Fourcade (2023) note that Netflix has over 2,000 different 'micro-communities' that it can then use to recommend future shows or future things that someone might want to watch. They note that '[y]our movie choices alter your position in this scheme and might in principle even alter the classificatory grid itself, creating a new category of viewer reflecting your idiosyncratic viewing practices' (Farrell and Fourcade 2023, 227). Real-time shifting of categories happens automatically, without the user reflecting on their category membership. Netflix clusters users into one of 2,000 malleable categories because they are seeking to create marketing instruments. There is an economies of scale element to algorithmic recommendation. Unique individuals are not worth the time and effort to indulge. Thousands of individuals, acting similarly with similar tastes, is a more appealing commercial product to package for those that want to understand consumer behaviour. Data brokers can package this 'aesthetic cluster' of potential customers to companies who see links between a Netflix cluster and their products. Hence the algorithm cannot just 'give you what you want' but must 'recommend what you should want'. To be grouped with tens of thousands requires this dynamic, emergent process where the category changes as consumer preferences change. What makes algorithmic categorization so much more effective and pernicious is that, while people have agency, their agency is limited when they do not know what they are acting upon.

In a scene from one of my favourite films, *Willy Wonka and the Chocolate Factory* (1971), the guests enter a room filled with giant geese laying eggs. Willy Wonka describes to the guests that the eggs pass through an 'Eggducated Eggdicator', designed to quickly sort 'eggs' based on their quality. When one of the guests (Veruca Salt) petulantly stands on the chute and falls through it, we are confirmed in our presumption that she was a 'bad egg'. But, just like our modern, proprietary algorithms, we never really know how it came to classify the eggs and what biases have been encoded into their decision calculus. There is an alternative universe where Veruca grows up and steers her petulant nature towards enthusiastic advocacy for a cause. The certitude and opacity of this fanciful predecessor to AI precludes us from ever finding out why 'eggs' are good or bad.

High-tech modernism is infinitely more capable of keeping users controlled through classification. In the 1960s and 1970s, spy agencies like the Stasi in Eastern Europe would go to great lengths to build nondescript listening devices to spy on its citizens. Now, the Internet of Things, sophisticated algorithms, and high-speed processing has created a world in which we can be categorized and re-categorized on the fly, without our knowledge and without the need to be rigidly monitored. Scott (1998) takes care to argue that citizens don't passively accept their categorization, they resist it. In fact, this is a massive challenge for authoritarian or even democratic states that want to know their citizens. If citizens resist categorization, that frustrates the goals of the rationalist state. Arendt (1951) drew a distinction between authoritarianism and totalitarianism. In authoritarian societies, one maintains one's autonomy and the latent potential to resist. In totalitarianism, subjects have 'bought in' to the illiberal project and do not know the difference between freedom and oppression. In the next chapter, I will expand upon this idea of a 'classification' logic.

2

The Politics of Optimization

The Mexican painter Diego Rivera, in defence of his controversial mural for the 1940 San Francisco World's Fair, entitled *Pan American Unity*, purportedly made the statement 'All art is propaganda ... All painters have been propagandists or else they have not been painters' (Whitney 2022). By 'propaganda,' Rivera likely meant that all artistic efforts, whether overtly political or not, convey value propositions, signifiers, and representations intended to communicate a point of view. Even art that seems banal or apolitical still carries underlying assumptions about what is good or just and what is not.

Similarly, Winner (1980) argued that technological artifacts – machines, computers, and so on – have social and political implications embedded in their design. The biases and value propositions of designers get transmitted into their creations. Winner interpreted 'technology' broadly, using as an example the development of the interstate highway system in the United States. He argued that by facilitating the building of highways through poor and minority neighbourhoods (disrupting their commercial centres while leaving white-majority and wealthy neighbourhoods intact) the legislation produced socioeconomic winners and losers.

Algorithms also carry *a politics*. Training data inevitably produces bias for data scientists. Crawford (2021) calls training data 'ground truth'. While the term carries multiple definitions in religious and agricultural contexts, ground truth refers to the pre-labelled training data from which supervised machine learning algorithms learn. Regardless of the type of training data used (images, words, sounds, policing records, geolocation data, and so on), they constitute an abstraction from reality because they do not capture all possible cases. This abstracted ground truth becomes the foundation for machine truth.

Human labour plays a significant role in labelling datasets, making the process subjective and prone to error. For example, in a dataset for a dog classifier, the decision of which images contain a dog is based on human judgement. Machines learn from people and people are prone to error.

This subjectivity can bring into question the objectivity of machine truth. Algorithmic models are trying to simplify complexity, presumably so we can act with greater insight or information. Crawford's concern is that we substitute this flawed machine truth for the messiness and contingency of the real world from which it emerges. Behind the seeming objectivity of the algorithm lies the subjective, socio-technical choices of humans. Machine truth has the imprimatur of scientific legitimacy, yet it is a kind of propaganda (whether intentional or not).

As an example, in the field of predictive policing, the application of data-driven algorithms has raised significant concerns regarding the perpetuation of racial biases and discriminatory practices. These algorithms, designed to optimize crime prevention and resource allocation, often rely on historical crime data as their primary input. However, this approach is inherently problematic as it fails to account for the systemic biases and discriminatory policing practices that have historically shaped these datasets (Egbert and Mann 2021). The algorithms, in their pursuit of optimization, may inadvertently incorporate and reinforce biases, such as the notion that certain racial or ethnic groups are more prone to criminal behaviour.

The use of such algorithms creates a self-reinforcing cycle of bias. When the system suggests increased policing in areas with higher minority populations based on historical data, it often leads to more arrests in those areas, hence validating the algorithm's predictions (Doucette et al 2021). This data-driven reinforcement, however, fails to accurately reflect the complex reality of crime patterns and their underlying causes. It neglects crucial factors such as socioeconomic conditions, systemic inequalities, and the effects of over-policing in certain communities (Davis et al 2022). As a result, these predictive policing models risk perpetuating and exacerbating existing racial disparities in the criminal justice system, highlighting the critical need for a more nuanced and contextually aware approach to data-driven decision-making in law enforcement.

Choices made about 'which label is applied to what case' shape our future perception of objects and concepts. This is particularly true with predictive policing. You might not be a 'suspect' in real life, but, if the ground truth points to your potential criminality, an entire set of institutions will be inclined to treat you as such and, potentially, you begin to see yourself as 'a suspect'. Public policy scholars are aware that policy interventions can impact the self-concept of the target. Bacher-Hicks and de la Campa (2020) found that young black men whose first contact with the state came in the form of New York's 'Stop and Frisk' law were 1.8 per cent less likely to complete high school and 2.5 per cent less likely to enrol in college than similarly situated teens not stopped by police.

These examples apply to our online engagement as well. Algorithms do not simply classify people into categories, they shape and reconstruct their identities. When we search for items, the recommendation algorithms interpret our aggregated choices as a form of ground truth. Algorithms are 'reification machines' that calcify a particular 'ground truth' in the minds of users. Take an example of a facial recognition algorithm attempting to classify by race. Race is an abstract, subjective concept that is falsely treated as if it can be captured and correctly labelled through visual cues translated into vector space features. In reality, there are a large number of 'edge cases' that, upon visual inspection, do not fit neatly into any category. This is because racial identification is partially subjective. There is a long tradition of individuals in the United States who could 'pass for white' but would self-identify as black and because of state miscegenation laws would be legally classified as black. One drop rule policies in several US states reflected the reality that systems (and people) impose labels on undeserving or unrepresented subjects, relying on ahistorical assumptions of universal taxonomies. Once deployed, these systems can amplify inequalities and lock in identities, under the guise of objectivity.

The optimization logic

How are algorithms 'reification machines'? If artifacts have politics, *optimization logic* is a clue to what kind of politics it has. Chiodo and Müller (2023) argue that even 'mathematical artifacts', such as algorithms, equations, and theorems, carry political weight. They emphasize that by understanding the interconnected nature of mathematical uses and their societal effects we can more effectively address the impact that mathematical artifacts have on society. In their paper, Chiodo and Müller highlight several ways in which maths is used for social purposes. They argue that prediction – central to many mathematical models – not only makes statements about future events but also alters those events, influencing the behaviour of those being predicted. Additionally, they note that mathematics, as a language, carries significant legitimacy and trustworthiness, giving axiomatic truths considerable power in society: 'Any prediction alters the state of the world, even when it is not acted on, as it increases our knowledge and potential for action. When acted on, predictions about systems involving human interaction can become self-fulfilling prophecies or self-destructive as they amplify or reduce certain behaviors' (Chiodo and Müller 2023, 2). A politics of optimization treats 'outliers', or 'edge cases', as barriers to effective prediction, not as cases to be better understood and inform revisions to the algorithm. A different politics would see outliers as containing information about the explanatory limits of a given model. Lieberman (2005) suggested treating the 'off the (linear estimator) line' in econometric modelling as a subject for in-depth case study. The information gleaned from understanding these outlier cases could help researchers better understand the issue of interest. The causal mechanism underlying the outlier case could be brought into the model, thereby improving its explanatory power. Machine learning algorithms work differently. The approach that underlies AI is fundamentally about discovering patterns in data, whether through adversarial networks, large language models, or other training-driven processes to improve prediction.

Supervised and unsupervised machine learning are two fundamental approaches in algorithmic classification. In unsupervised learning, the algorithm receives data that is not labelled. The task for the algorithm is to find the underlying patterns in the data without prior training. These approaches involve clustering, dimensionality reduction, and anomaly detection. With unsupervised learning, the algorithm can uncover insights that would be impossible for humans to achieve. The patterns, however, are not readily interpretable to humans. For example, in an anomaly detection, the algorithm will identify outlier cases but, since it was not trained by humans, there is no easy means of interpreting why a case is an outlier. The task is not understanding why the outlier is behaving as it is, but rather the objective is to identify it as anomalous for its own sake. For prediction models, the ultimate goal for the data scientist is to reduce the cost function (error rate) of the model. The cost function is a mathematical formula that determines how well a machine learning model performs in accurately predicting the outcomes on a given dataset. The goal of the data scientist is to reduce the distance between the predicted values and the actual values.

In supervised learning, researchers train an algorithm on a labelled dataset that includes both independent variables (features) and dependent variables (outcomes). After testing the trained model on part of the dataset, the algorithm learns to label on its own, essentially learning how to predict or classify new, unseen cases. This approach is used in a variety of applications: image classification, spam detection, and financial analysis. A key challenge for the researcher is dealing with cases that do not seem to fit the pattern. A case that is not well predicted by the model reduces the overall cost function (increasing the error rate). The presence of these outlier cases reduces the predictive power of existing models on current data, but, more importantly, it impedes the ability of the model to predict future outcomes. This leaves the data scientist with a problem: if you 'brute force' the outlier to fit the pattern, you run the risk of overfitting the model to the training data and reducing its usefulness in predicting future cases. When a model becomes too closely tied to the training data, it becomes less able to generalize to new, unseen data. Conversely, if a model ignores too many outliers, it also reduces the predictive power of the model (it also may be a clue to the researcher that they need to collect more data).

Rather than seek to understand the outlier, data scientists often employ debugging techniques to 'reduce the cost function' of the algorithmic model. Debugging, in the context of machine learning, involves taking your model to another dataset to uncover where it might be failing. A common approach is to compare the performance of the model on the training set to that of a separate debugging set, allowing you to pinpoint weaknesses and tweak parameters for better performance.

One core debugging task is to tweak 'hyperparameters'. Hyperparameters are analogous to a 'coarseness setting on a meat grinder' (Kozyrkov 2022) that you can adjust to change how the model processes data. Each algorithm comes with its own set of hyperparameters – learning rates, batch sizes, temperature settings for exploration vs. exploitation, and so on. The process involves iterating through different hyperparameter configurations to find the one that delivers optimal performance (that is, reduces the cost function). This can be done manually but, increasingly, automated methods like grid search, random search, or Bayesian optimization are used to find the best hyperparameter set efficiently (Kozyrkov 2022).

Most supervised learning algorithms involve 'gradient descent' – an iterative process where the algorithm calculates the partial derivative of the cost function (error rate) for each parameter (the gradient), which indicates the direction of the steepest increase in the cost function. The algorithm then, in a stepwise process, adjusts the weights for each parameter in the model, in the opposite direction of the gradient, incrementally moving towards a lower cost function. You can think of it as a hiker trying to find the fastest way down a mountain with many unseen peaks and valleys. The 'learning rate' determines the size of the movement (steps) the algorithm takes in its pursuit. The learning rate is one of the more critical hyperparameters since a large learning rate runs the risk of overshooting the optimal solution, while one that is overly cautious takes too much computational time to arrive at the optimal point or the 'minima'.

In machine learning, however, there is a distinction between the 'global minima' and 'local minima'. The global minima is the lowest possible value of the cost function across the entire vector space. The local minima, by contrast, is the lowest point of the cost function in the 'neighbourhood' in which the algorithm is working. Returning to the hiker in a mountain range example, the height at any point can be thought of as the cost function in the gradient descent process. If you were to go hiking in that range to find the lowest point, you would be constrained by where you happened to be within the mountain range. The local minima is analogous to a valley or depression that is lower than the immediate surroundings but is not necessarily the lowest point overall. If you were seeking the lowest point in a mountain range, you would be unable to tell if the current valley you were in was the lowest point in the entire range. There are likely even lower points in the range that you do not know about. Data scientists weigh the costs of pursuing the global minima since often a local minima performs reasonably well for most optimization tasks. A 'good enough' local minima is what researchers seek.

The consequences of optimization logic

The logic of finding the local minima at a given learning rate is not just a machine learning problem but a cultural ethos. We live in a culture of optimization. From countless blogs and TED Talks promising to increase personal efficiency to books like Tim Ferriss' early 2000s bestsellers *The 4-Hour Workweek* (2007) and *The 4-Hour Body* (2010), or James Clear's successful book *Atomic Habits* (2018), optimization is a pervasive theme in our culture. Embedded in the ethos of 'hustle culture' is the imperative to 'do as much as you can with as little effort as possible'. Social media platforms are overrun with influencers seeking to gain an audience by promising to increase the efficiency and productivity of followers through 'lifehacks'. This had pervaded global culture to such an extent that the top TikTok influencer of 2023 was a Senegalese-Italian named Khaby Lame who regularly pokes fun at 'overly complicated life hacks', like using odd contraptions to put on socks. His lampooning of 'optimization culture' has earned him over 160 million followers. His success is testament to the ubiquity of 'optimization' culture online.

This cultural fixation with optimization is not just about improving efficiency. It is a value system that shapes how we interact with the world, often reinforcing social and political norms under the guise of neutrality and efficiency. As McKelvey and Neves (2021, 95) put it: 'Optimization has become a keyword, an underexplored cultural and political process, and a critical concept for understanding our highly technologized world. We define optimization as a form of calculative decision-making, deeply embedded in legitimating institutions and media that seek to implement optimal social and technical practices in real time.' In recent years, scholars have shed light on how cultural production on social media platforms has fostered what Morris et al (2021) call a 'cultural disposition' towards optimization, especially in terms of engagement and monetization. They point out that each platform – whether Spotify, YouTube, or Apple – creates its own logic of optimization. This cultural optimization involves treating cultural products as data and content, produced specifically to be visible to the myriad discovery engines and interfaces through which content must circulate in today's digital platforms.

Morris et al (2021, 163) argue that platform optimization logics cultivate a 'calculative mindset' among content creators. Artists are increasingly encouraged to view their work not as artistic expression but as data and code that needs to be aligned with the algorithm to be seen. This shift in perspective not only alters marketing strategies but also transforms content itself, as well as the nature of the creators behind it.

Artists modify cultural products to accommodate the dictates of the algorithm. Musicians change lyrics and titles to manipulate traffic, optimize song structures to grab listeners' attention early and hold it for at least 30 seconds to extract royalties, and shape the sound of their music to be discoverable by algorithms and users curating 'mood-based playlists' (Morris et al 2021, 165). This practice of artists trying to discern what the algorithm likes rather than developing their own artistic voice is very akin to a gradient descent algorithm in a stepwise fashion attempting to find the local minima.

Hallinan (2023) analysed 200 YouTube videos across various categories and found that creators optimized their content to the algorithm, making it more accessible and discoverable for viewers. She refers to this as 'cultural optimization', distinct from the 'formal optimization' content creators use to drive engagement through strategies like using 'clickbait' titles or modifying thumbnails (Hallinan 2023, 1–2). Formal optimization involves creators measuring, engineering, and designing elements of their content to make it more searchable and valuable on platforms like YouTube. In a sense, artists are taking it upon themselves to 'reduce the cost function'.

The more intriguing aspect of Hallinan's (2023) study is what she calls 'value optimization', where creators employ specific rhetorical strategies that they believe align with the normative values incentivized by the platform (2). These strategies include an emphasis on aesthetics and functionality, which prioritizes personalization and consumption over other values. Creators are encouraged to avoid strong judgements that might alienate viewers, instead focusing on opinion and adopting what Trillò et al (2021, 892) call 'aestheticized consumption'. In this process, every value position is 'transformed into visual representations of goods for consumption' (Trillò et al 2021, 893). Trillò et al (2021, 893) note a number of examples of this phenomenon on Instagram: 'Sustainability becomes visualizable mainly in terms of green marketing; Tradition becomes associated with products like costumes and food; and Health doesn't involve medical doctors or surgical masks, but gym subscriptions and green smoothies to achieve a toned body'. In this model, creators rarely invoke cultural hierarchies, preferring the autonomy associated with amateur assessments on social media. This commercial-friendly strategy allows them to cater to large audiences without stepping into contentious debates, promoting personalization and broad appeal over critical or community-driven standards. The focus becomes monetization and the conversion of art and aesthetics into lifestyle consumption patterns.

This focus on personalized aesthetics is not problematic per se. Cochrane (2021) argues for cultivating aesthetic value to find lasting significance in the world, which may be more reliable than moral value. According to him, moral value can easily be shattered by evils like violence or injustice, but aesthetic value transcends these forces. He suggests that aesthetics can help us see beauty even in seemingly immoral or ugly things. For example, a rotting animal carcass may initially seem grotesque, but, when viewed in a broader context, it can be seen as part of the natural process of decay that nourishes a forest and constitutes a form of rebirth. Aesthetic appreciation can either disturb us or connect us to a transcendent order.

What becomes of aesthetics when it is controlled by algorithm? Historically, artistic creation has always considered monetary value and elite taste. The shift to algorithmically informed aesthetics moves us away from an appreciation of novelty, aesthetic innovation, or the cultivation of individual voice towards consumer preferences and audience engagement. This disincentivizes art that 'pushes the envelope' and is detached from how it might be consumed or presented to an audience. It creates an 'optimization' of art that preferences algorithmically driven predictability over experimentation.

Music critic Ted Gioia (2022) points out that 70 per cent of the US platform streaming market now consists of old songs. While the decline in new music production is due to multiple factors, Gioia identifies a key cause: the lack of innovation and risk-taking in the music industry. Pop music, for instance, has seen a decrease in key changes since 2012 (Dalla Riva 2022). User preferences for the familiar, which prioritizes familiar music, combined with the datafication of tastes, has made user tastes predictable. Platforms like Spotify prioritize older, familiar songs, and, as a result, artists are pressured to replicate those familiar sounds to fit within recommendation algorithms.

Gioia also notes the increasing use of music as 'furniture', background noise in a society marked by accelerated multitasking and attention deprivation. This familiarity not only limits the development of new talent and ideas but also reflects what Gioia calls the music industry's lost faith in the transformative power of new music. He writes:

> The people running the music industry have lost confidence in new music. They won't admit it publicly – that would be like the priests of Jupiter and Apollo in ancient Rome admitting that their gods are dead … The safest path is often the most dangerous. If you pursue a strategy – whether in business or your personal life – that avoids all risk, you might flourish in the short run, but you will flounder over the long term. (Gioia 2022)

Pelley (2017) makes a similar claim, decrying 'technosolutionism' as applied to music discovery through algorithm. The algorithm leads users to rely on playlists to discover music, what she calls 'lean back listening', which leads to a less engaged relationship to music. This is part of what Pelley calls the 'totalizing ambitions' of platforms like Spotify, Pandora, and YouTube Music, which control every aspect of the music industry, from creation to distribution to discovery. The effect of this ambition is the optimization of cultural production for consumption. This erodes independent artistry, risks creative stagnation, and incentivizes creative industries to become more focused on minimizing risk and maximizing familiarity rather than fostering innovation and artistic discovery. As Gioia (2022) concludes, 'music company executives in 1955 had no idea that rock 'n' roll would soon sweep away everything in its wake'. The relentless drive towards optimization today may prevent the next musical innovation from taking root.

A similar process exists in game and app development. Morris et al (2021) argue that, while early digital game development (early console games, arcade titles) were constrained by hardware limitations dictating design, modern game development is constrained by game distribution platforms like Steam, which popularized the 'freemium model' that emphasizes monetizing in-game items. This shift does not enhance the gaming experience but allows game development to engage in 'ex-post optimization', where developers use key performance indicators to determine the amount of time users spent playing the game and the amount of money users spent on in-game experiences (buying avatars, extra lives, or game artifacts).

Morris et al (2021) find similar dynamics in the app development space. App stores, like the Apple iOS store and Google Play, are determinative of an app's success. Early developers became adept at search engine optimization (SEO) to increase the popularity of their apps. In recent years, an SEO industry has cropped up that goes beyond keyword searches. As Morris et al (2021, 169) write, '[s]earch visibility is now just one part of a suite of optimization offerings, including tactics for improving the number of successful installs (conversion optimization), preview video and screenshot optimization, marketing copy optimization, and sentiment analysis'. The effort to gain traction on app stores produces a circular logic where app developers try to discern how the algorithm will reward them, and app stores look out for developers seeking to 'game' the algorithm to push substandard or malicious apps onto their platform. As Morris et al (2021, 169–70) describe it:

> Optimization, then, is circular; it has an impact on cultural production but at the same time culture profoundly impacts optimization. ASO [app store optimization] companies and app publishers react to the metrics and features that platforms provide, and platforms react to how ASO companies and app publishers try to game or subvert their algorithmic and editorial processes. App stores 'optimize' for their own needs (i.e., eliminate spoof apps, profit, interface updates, etc.). As they make these changes, they set new terms for how cultural producers might then need to optimize their cultural commodities. ASO companies then present their optimization solutions as a means for app publishers to stand out in these crowded markets.

This tendency away from novelty and innovation towards cultural sameness through personalized aesthetics also exists in the built environment.

Chayka (2024) points out how the presumed individualism of the algorithmic society creates a global ubiquity that standardizes physical interior and exterior spaces. Travel and entertainment platforms like Yelp and Instagram steer users towards venues with highly rated aesthetics. In turn, businesses all over the world 'optimize their aesthetic' to rise in the algorithmic ranking on these platforms. This produces a pernicious feedback loop, where interiors systematically move towards a non-threatening, modally pleasant design. Chayka (2024, 6) calls this phenomenon 'AirSpace' – spaces that seamlessly adopt a similar style: a bright, open concept, minimalist aesthetic that may change over time, but is designed to cater primarily to a Western, affluent demographic.

The editors of the literary magazine N+1 (2023) recently published an editorial on what they call the 'new ugliness', characterized by bland, uninspiring architecture, cropping up in American cities. They call these new structures 'cardboard modernism': cheap, unadventurous structures made inexpensively with flimsy materials and lacking in character or visual appeal. They decry how this homogeneous aesthetic is spreading across cities leading to a phenomenon they call 'non-place' where cities increasingly look the same. They blame this lack of adventuresomeness in design on the algorithm:

> [A]ll that is solid melts into sameness, such that smart home devices resemble the buildings they surveil, which in turn look like the computers on which they were algorithmically engineered, which resemble the desks on which they sit, which, like the sofas at the coworking space around the corner, put the mid in fake midcentury modern. And all of it is bound by the commandment of planned obsolescence, which decays buildings even as it turns phones into bricks. (N+1 2023)

The effects of optimization culture might be aesthetically displeasing to literary and art critics, but they have a democratic legitimacy to them. We may complain about the effects of algorithms on our lives, but we do not reject the technologies that facilitate them. As Baudrillard (1981) reminds us, we just might prefer the sterile, predictable 'simulacra' of the Italian bistro in Disney's Epcot Center to the contingent unpredictability of a real-world Italian bistro. In the next chapter, I will discuss the consequences for politics of this optimization logic and expand upon the idea of an algorithmic contract akin to a social contract in political theory that helps us understand the legitimacy we give algorithms in governing our lives.

3

The Problem for Democracy

If algorithms optimize culture, then to what purpose should they be optimized when it comes to the state? In this chapter, I lay out three different potential approaches for optimizing algorithms towards the goals of the state: a 'republic of virtue' approach, a 'preservation of the self' approach and a 'preservation of rights' approach. I then move onto talking about how, in the United States, the overwhelming emphasis of tech-activists is for algorithms to be optimized towards the preservation of rights. I briefly discuss the differences between US and European approaches and explain why the preservation of rights approach can be incomplete.

A 'republic of virtue' optimization

Civic Republican political theory posits that the state has an affirmative role to play in promoting civic virtue (Sandel 1988). If we can agree on what civic virtue is, we could optimize algorithms to promote good citizenship. Adherents of a classical view would build on the Aristotelian concept of 'telos' which suggests that everything is built with a natural purpose. A teleological view suggests that embedded within all humans is a natural inclination towards certain virtues, such as preserving life, educating the young, and preferring order – much like a watch is designed to tell time. If a watch fails to fulfil its natural purpose, it is considered a watch in need of repair. Similarly, if humans fail to fulfil their telos, they are not achieving their moral purpose.

This idea implies that humans can be evaluated based on their alignment with this purpose. Correspondingly, algorithms could be trained to encourage virtuous behaviour. Feeds might be populated with examples of people engaging in such behaviour or show people punished for being unvirtuous. This is the starting point for philosopher Shannon Vallor. Her work on virtue ethics in relation to technology and AI has been influential in the field. In her seminal book, *Technology and the Virtues: A Philosophical Guide to a Future Worth Wanting*, Vallor (2016) proposes a framework of 'technomoral virtues' to guide the ethical development and use of emerging technologies. Vallor identifies twelve technomoral virtues that she deems particularly necessary for navigating the digital age: honesty, self-control, humility, justice, courage, empathy, care, civility, flexibility, perspective, magnanimity, and wisdom. She recognizes the need to make these virtues flexible and adaptable to different contexts. As such, she draws on a range of moral traditions – Aristotelian, Confucian, and Buddhist – to develop technomoral ethics. She prioritizes the cultivation of 'technomoral wisdom' (Vallor 2016, 11) that helps individuals navigate the complexities of technology. While acknowledging the challenges of finding a common morality in a pluralist society, she nonetheless insists that societies need a grounding in some value ethic to combat the 'acute techno social opacity' of technological systems (Vallor 2016, 23).

The challenge of 'optimizing for ethics' in a pluralist liberal society is finding a shared set of value propositions. The origins of Aristotelian virtue are that the state has affirmative responsibilities to cultivate an elite with elevated capacity to reason that could rule over the 'unwise'. Civil society confers obligations and duties to each individual based on their social position. In *Politics*, Aristotle proposes that the role of the state is to encourage its citizens to live a good (in other words, virtuous) life (Lord 2013, 17–24). For him, virtue is based on a common understanding that each individual has a role (telos) to play in establishing a harmonious order. Such a society would emphasize order and duty over individual autonomy and disagreements.

Contemporary conservative scholars in the United States, like law professor Adrian Vermuele (2020) and political theorist Patrick Deneen (2019), critique liberalism for over-emphasizing individual autonomy, failing to guide individuals towards 'the virtues'. This deeper crisis in modernity requires the involvement of the state to promote a specific Judeo-Christian conception of virtue. Although they do not discuss the use of algorithms and surveillance technology, the 'optimization task' for these scholars would involve using algorithmic surveillance to make subjects legible to determine if they are indeed fulfilling their telos. Given the ambitions of conservative nationalist groups in the United States and Europe, it is not far-fetched to envision a scenario where algorithms are trained on vast amounts of user data to steer users towards a republic of virtue. We see echoes of this in China's construction of a social credit system to reward virtuous behaviour and punish transgression.

A 'preservation of the self' optimization

A modern view is that a 'republic of virtue' is too constricting of individuals who can use their reason and their agency to determine the good. Enforcing a view of the good on citizens undermines their autonomy and individuality.

Enlightenment thinkers, like Hobbes, challenged the view of an externally imposed societal telos, arguing that the 'natural' state of humans is to survive in a world where humans are self-interested and in a 'war of every man against everyman' (Hobbes 1967, 150). In this view, we live in constant fear of our physical safety, and virtue cultivation becomes irrelevant in a world where survival is paramount. Taking this further, Hobbes suggests that a 'good state' has an all-powerful hegemon that prevents widespread violence in a natural world that is 'nasty, brutish and short' (Hobbes 1967, 97). He redefines natural law as the desire for self-preservation, proposing that the state's role is not to create civil society but to 'preserve the self' (Hobbes 1967, 168). In such a world, the optimization task is not how to help individuals and societies live virtuously but to 'predict' and 'monitor' subjects through algorithmic surveillance to ensure they do not harm others.

Indeed, this is the way much of the optimization task is understood by aspects of modern states. In recent years, the use of advanced technologies for surveillance and public safety has become increasingly prevalent among governments, security agencies, and law enforcement bodies worldwide. For the last two decades, law enforcement agencies in the United States have engaged in 'predictive policing', which utilizes historical crime data and machine learning algorithms to allocate resources to potential crime hotspots. Agencies also engage in social media monitoring to identify patterns and potential threats (Trottier and Fuchs 2014). Finally, facial recognition technology has become a key element of modern surveillance systems, particularly for anti-terrorism efforts in airports and border crossings (Warren and Mavroudi 2011). The basis for much of the modern algorithmic security state is 'anomaly detection'. These efforts often use unsupervised machine learning techniques to identify unusual patterns or behaviours. Anomaly detection efforts are applied to crowd monitoring at large public events, to protect critical infrastructure and to detect fraud.

The challenge with a preservation of rights perspective is the undermining of civil rights and liberties. Lyon (2014) argues that we are becoming a 'surveillance society', where we willingly give up personal privacy and civil liberties for the appearance of safety. Yet entrusting the state with significant power to 'know' citizens raises questions of accountability (Diakopoulos 2020). A challenge with Hobbes' view of a state which prioritizes 'preserving the self' was the lack of accountability. Giving a centralized authority unlimited power to maintain order creates risks to civil liberties if the hegemon decided to act arbitrarily or capriciously against 'enemies of the state'.

A 'preservation of rights' optimization

This view of 'surveillance' algorithms represents a tragic vision of human nature rooted in assumptions of human selfishness and inherent violence.

By contrast, other thinkers, such as Locke, offered a more hopeful vision. For them, humans in the state of nature were neutral, a *tabula rasa* that could become violent or peaceful, depending on the circumstances. Locke believed that humans left the state of nature to guarantee their 'natural rights', not to avoid a war of all against all. This view of human nature is deeply rooted in enlightenment individualism and the potential of human beings to improve and govern themselves (Locke 1996 [1689], 33–36).

In the 19th and 20th centuries, this rights-based view evolved into one less associated with the individual's potential to use reason to self-govern and instead saw self-government as an axiomatic principle. The Kantian enlightenment 'kingdom of ends' principle that establishes the self as intrinsically worthy of dignity replaced a 'republic of virtue' perspective that prioritized the cultivation of virtue and civic wisdom. The mass violence in the 20th century reinforced Isaiah Berlin's (2014) belief that no state-ideological project was sustainable because it always led to violence against dissenters, hence we are left with the 'negative liberty' of a minimal state that protects individual freedom. Coupled with market capitalism, this meant the individual's 'right to consume'. A 'rights-based' view of algorithmic optimization means algorithms should serve individual needs with minimal interference from the state.

The challenge of regulating algorithms in the United States

A minimal state view helps us understand why the United States has minimally regulated social media and engagement algorithms. Parties differ regarding what it means to 'preserve rights' on private discourse platforms. This difference boils down to either 'the truth is being concealed from you through algorithmic removal' or 'the truth is being concealed from you through algorithmic amplification'. In the case of amplification, parties want stricter content moderation to police misinformation, but challenges abound in this regard. How do you optimize for policing misinformation? It is often difficult to know what constitutes 'false information'. We are not privy to absolute certainty about the world. We can rely on the 'best available science', but the nature of empirical science is not to declare 'absolute truth'. Even if we can identify scientific consensus, there is debate about how we go about correcting the misinformation. Prematurely removing dissenting views might rightly inspire outrage against people who sincerely believe in the dissent.

Conversely, others want a 'neutral' environment where discourse is lightly regulated under the guise of preserving free expression. In this view, people should be allowed to judge for themselves whether content is 'misinformation' or not or to express illiberal and intolerant views. In a June

2024 US Supreme Court case, *Murthy v. Missouri*, Republican state attorney generals sued the Biden administration for allegedly pressuring social media companies to censor what the administration considered to be COVID-19 and vaccine misinformation. The Supreme Court ruled 6–3 in favour of the administration, citing that there was no direct evidence of coercion. The fact that the plaintiffs lost in this case has not deterred the view among the right wing in the United States that social media platforms are hostile to conservative viewpoints and are deliberately silencing political views. As a result, social media platforms have moved in the direction of 'neutrality'. Elon Musk's purchase of Twitter and Mark Zuckerberg's revelation that he felt remorse over 'caving in' to the Biden administration's pressure to more stringently monitor COVID-19 information (Korte 2024) are two examples of this shift towards minimal algorithmic moderation for misinformation.

In other parts of the world, governments have taken more proactive efforts to restrict platforms and algorithms. The European Union (EU) has adopted 'conditional immunity' laws (through the Digital Services Act 2022) that require platforms to take aggressive steps to remove illicit content and to be transparent in their engagement with users. Individual European nations have adopted or are considering legislation with similar levels of accountability to the EU's laws. Examples are the UK's Online Safety Act (2023) and Germany's Network Enforcement Act (NetzDG) (2017) legislation. Non-European nations like India require social media companies to employ 'grievance officers' to address user concerns (Singh and Singh 2022). A number of nations (Vietnam, Turkey, Pakistan) are adopting data localization initiatives (a requirement that data be kept within a nation's borders (Masinsin 2025).

In contrast, the United States remains deadlocked on how to proceed. Members of Congress have been satisfied with Committee hearings in which they berate major tech company CEOs like Mark Zuckerberg (Meta CEO), Jack Dorsey (Twitter CEO from 2015 to 2021), and Sundai Pichai (Google CEO). By summer of 2024, Congress appeared to be ready to move on online protections for children. The Senate passed the Kids Online Safety Act, which would establish a 'duty of care' standard for tech companies if minors are likely to use their platforms. Platforms would be obligated to 'prevent and mitigate' children's access to harmful content (suicide, eating disorders, substance abuse, sexual exploitation, and so on). Platforms would also be required to give minors options to protect their information, disable addictive product features, and opt out of personalized recommendation algorithms (Ortutay 2024). While the legislation passed the US Senate in the summer of 2024, the legislature was stalled in the House of Representatives at the end of 2024 with dim prospects for passage. The power of the technology lobby is in no small part responsible for this, but it is not the entirety of the story.

What does the preservation of rights mean on social media platforms?

The inability to act on regulating algorithms at the national level in the United States is rooted in the debate over what the preservation of rights in online spaces means. Social media platforms are largely private. Even if individual platforms purport to be, in Jack Dorsey's words, a 'public sphere' (Dorsey 2019), few take that as a serious pronouncement. Users post on social media sites because they feel they have a 'right' and a desire to speak their minds and this is a place where they can do so. But in the American context, there is a distinction between rights and liberties. Liberty places no obligations on the state other than a prohibition on interference from individuals exercising their liberties. The second amendment right to bear arms in the United States might be a good example. A right is one that requires government involvement to ensure the right is enjoyed. In the US context, the broad range of rights that apply to an expedient jury of one's peers or access to legal counsel and due process requires a court system to be in place for that right to be exercised.

Is the 'right to exercise voice' on social media a right or a liberty? We think of it as liberty, something that does not require action from the state but is inherently granted to citizens. But on social media, the discourse environment is not neutral, it is algorithmically mediated. Sociologist Chris Bail (2021, 66) makes a persuasive case that users receive social media content 'through a prism' that algorithmically distorts our perceptions of the world and in turn our own perceptions of how we fit into this distorted reality. In this 'prismatic' environment, can we say that we are able to exercise our right to voice? The nature of the preservation of rights view is that people are capable of discernment and can determine for themselves truth from fiction. But does that assumption hold in an algorithmically altered environment? Are freedoms preserved if algorithm distorts one's ability to make good judgements?

Recent research has highlighted the potentially harmful effects of social media engagement algorithms on users' mental health and social well-being. Algorithms, designed to maximize user engagement and time spent on platforms, have been found to amplify content that is emotionally charged, controversial, or sensationalistic. Brady et al (2023) propose that algorithms exploit human social learning biases by amplifying what they term 'PRIME' information (prestigious, ingroup, moral, and emotional), leading to increased polarization and the spread of misinformation. This algorithmic amplification can result in users developing skewed perceptions of social reality, with studies suggesting it may contribute to 'false polarization' and exaggerated perceptions of political divides (Brady et al 2023, 947). Furthermore, the constant exposure to curated, often idealized, content has been linked to negative impacts on mental health. Surveys indicate users report feeling exhausted and unhappy with the over-representation of extreme or controversial content in their feeds (Brady et al 2023, 955).

Brubaker (2022) challenges the idea that Internet culture has been a net good for democracy by expanding the range of people who can participate in cultural production. Brubaker argues that rather than 'democratizing culture', we are experiencing a phase of digital hyperconnectivity that provides us with a tsunami of cultural products, nominally distinguishable from one another. This is only increasing with the advent of AI tools that promise to help 'creators' develop cultural artifacts with limited technical skill to profit from a trend. For culture to truly become 'democratic', Brubaker argues its production would have to be decoupled from market motives and, more importantly, decoupled from the algorithms that govern the circulation (and optimization) of cultural products.

Despite the negative consequences of Internet culture on our mental health and social relations, we are increasingly willing participants. The global adoption of social media has seen a steady increase over the past decade. According to Pew data, there are now 5.17 billion active social media users worldwide, representing 63.7 per cent of the global population (St. Aubin and Liedke 2024b). This marks a substantial growth from 2.07 billion users in 2015, more than doubling in less than a decade. The year-over-year increase remains notable, with 282 million new users joining social media platforms in 2024, equating to an annualized growth rate of 5.8 per cent (Blog2Social 2024). The average user engages with 6.7 different social media platforms, spending approximately 2 hours and 20 minutes daily on these networks (Meltwater 2025). Platforms like Facebook, YouTube, Instagram, TikTok, and WhatsApp have become a daily part of global life. If the internet is making us isolated and miserable, we are willing participants in our misery making. Why are we doing this to ourselves?

The Hobbesian preservation of self-view posits that humans are power-seeking creatures. They desire not only material goods but also intangible rewards like fame, respect, notoriety, praise, and security. Social media presents an opportunity to intentionally distort reality in ways that will confuse or harm others for personal gain. In the state of nature, which Hobbes famously describes as 'nasty, brutish, and short' (Hobbes 1967, 97), life is governed by constant threat. We can see a 'public sphere' like Twitter (now X) as less of a discourse environment and more of a 'war of all against all' to attain status, wealth, and power. If unregulated, unmoderated social media is akin to a 'war of all against all', then few people exercise voice out of fear of criticism, verbal attack, ostracization, or, in rare cases, physical violence. Hobbes contends that we all seek material wealth and/or psychological status (respect, notoriety, fame, and so on). Even if we do not want these things for ourselves or are not willing to be violent to attain or protect them, we live in constant subjugation to those who would and do. This perpetual fear diminishes human life. For Hobbes, the war of all against all can only be stopped by a 'visible power to keep (us) in awe' (Hobbes 1967, 128). With social media platforms, no such power exists. The engagement algorithm is an active perpetuator of a war of all against all, suggesting content that promotes violence, sexuality, exploitation, and other forms of harm. In the United States, we have a Lockean system of government that fails to regulate an increasingly Hobbesian public sphere.

The world before social media recommendation algorithms did not feel like a 'war of all against all' (Hobbes 1967, 150). Humans were still capable of harming one another, but there were community norms and obligations that constrained the worst content. Users could block, report, or ignore noxious accounts. Early social media platforms differed significantly from their modern counterparts that employ sophisticated engagement algorithms. In the early days of social networking, platforms like Myspace and early versions of Facebook presented content in chronological order with minimal algorithmic intervention. Users would see posts from their friends and follow pages in the order they were published, creating a more organic and unfiltered experience. Content visibility was primarily determined by the time of posting rather than engagement metrics. As a result, users were exposed to a more diverse range of content and opinions from their network.

The absence of complex engagement algorithms also meant that viral content spread more organically through genuine user interest and sharing, rather than through being amplified by algorithmically driven systems. Additionally, early social media platforms had less sophisticated targeting capabilities for advertisements, leading to a less personalized but potentially more serendipitous user experience. This era of social media was characterized by users having a greater sense of control over their feed content and a more straightforward relationship between users and the platform. But it was also potentially less engaging. Because engagement algorithms and the rise of smartphones grew in parallel, it is hard to know the extent to which the increase of social media platform use is the result of engagement algorithms or the rise of smartphone capabilities.

Engagement algorithms present us with an *augmented state of nature*, offering users a prismatic view of the world that is more 'nasty, brutish and short' than it is in reality. We are then given the platform to opine on this brutishness, either approving of it through likes and reposts or commenting on the brutishness, giving us license to engage in moral outrage (Crockett 2017). The tradition of American individualism where everyone believes they have a right to offer their opinion because they are 'equal' in their person means that there is an overabundance of voice online. There is no shortage of social media users (and bots) ready to excoriate bad behaviour, inadvertently amplifying it and incentivizing more of it.

The ambivalent nature of online interactions can blur the lines between genuine engagement and trolling, often leading to unintended amplification of problematic content (Phillips and Milner 2017). Bad actors exploit media manipulation tactics, leveraging both human psychology and platform mechanics to gain visibility (Marwick and Lewis 2017). False news spreads faster and more broadly than truth on social media, suggesting that the very nature of provocative or controversial content makes it more likely to be shared (Vosoughi et al 2018). The result is an online environment that confirms a dismal view of human nature. More importantly, optimization culture does to politics what it did for arts and culture, a convergence on the part of social media users to adjust to the algorithm when discussing politics. In this case, users converge in predictable ways towards the outrageous. An example might be the countless Twitter/X posts from United States congresspersons from the Republican Party that feature a family Christmas card where each member is holding an assault rifle. This recycling of tropes, what we recognize as 'memes', through likes, comments, or shares amplifies one political classification.

This poses challenges for a rights-based approach. If we do live in an augmented state of nature, most of us do so willingly, or at least begrudgingly. Most users are entertained by, if not addicted to, the augmented state of nature. Even if we have private concerns, we would not want a 'lawgiver' hegemon to police 'harms' on social media. Tech companies would argue that we have the tools to block content and to train the algorithm to 'give us what we want'. In 2018, Facebook found that changing their algorithm to feature higher quality content led to less user engagement. As a result, they modified their algorithm to feature posts that were divisive, sensational, or controversial. The company did this despite internal concerns about the impact on the spread of misinformation, raising political tensions, and negatively impacting youth mental health (Hao 2021). Facebook's efforts at addressing these issues ran up against the drop in engagement when they modified the algorithm away from the harmful content. How do we make sense of our love–hate relationship to the algorithms in our lives and what are the effects? I turn to this in the next chapter.

4

The Algorithmic Contract and its Discontents

Our online lives produce an abundance of anxiety (and an anxiety of abundance). The neoliberal promise of a 'library on your desktop' creates possibility and dread at the same time. Sartre (2007, 44) is famous for saying 'I can always choose, but I must know that if I do not choose, that is still a choice'. How does one know one is 'choosing correctly' online? We have not mapped out the contours of this complex relationship with the online world. Freedom in the age of data abundance might be less a freedom of access, and more a freedom to be relieved of the burden of choosing.

The algorithmic contract promises this world of unlimited online possibility. It is true that online tools not only give us a myriad of examples of 'how we can be', but also provide the opportunity to narrowcast their own version of being. We can try on different 'experiments in living' for size and make our experiences public. But that promise comes with the need to wade through vast amounts of nonsense. The Internet presents us with a real-world Library of Babel (Borges 1998), a fictional library that contains an infinite array of equal-sized books with every conceivable combination of letters, spaces, and punctuation marks. The library houses every book that could possibly be written, the vast majority of which would be gibberish. This constant churn of lifestyles and opinions on our social media feeds is akin to a Library of Babel that we need to make comprehensible.

Eran Fisher differentiates between the 'toil of labor' in the 20th century driven by the necessity of work in capitalism, to a 'toil of choice' (Fisher in Jarow 2022) today where an abundant online information/entertainment environment creates anxieties that can be lessened by allowing the algorithm to choose for us. With the toil of labor one might still have existential anxiety, but the all-encompassing nature of labouring serves as something of a distraction from the more existential. In pre-modern societies, there is not much value in speculating upon possible selves because the chances of realizing a different self is limited. The toil of choice provided by online tools amplifies Sartre's (1946, 44) 'paradox of choice'. This toil provokes existential anxiety because the algorithm and the social media platform give the impression that 'all things are possible', and now you must choose among them. The amount of choice we are subjected to in an era of information abundance is overwhelming. In popular culture, this gets expressed by the term FOMO (fear of missing out).

The trade-off Fisher envisions is that, by ceding this toil of choice to the algorithm, we are relieved from the anxiety of choosing and our information environment is made more comprehensible. By ceding our autonomy to the algorithm to relieve the toil of choice, however, our conception of freedom shifts. Instead of our sense of autonomy emanating from within, autonomy becomes externalized – a *freedom from without* (Fisher in Jarow 2022). The enlightenment view of individual freedom rooted in self-determination and self-mastery is replaced with a freedom externally dependent upon the algorithm to structure our choices. Our freedom becomes determined by the algorithm. This freedom is not the Kantian 'kingdom of ends' (Kant 2017), but more of a Hobbesian cognitive/psychological freedom (Hobbes 1967) to be sheltered from the anxiety of choice. The prospect that I could be wrong in my worldview creates great anxiety. By asking the algorithm to free us from the toil of choice, we ask the algorithm to structure our data environment in ways that relieves our burden. This becomes freedom. As a result, Fisher says, we lose our 'emancipatory interest', or the desire to free ourselves from outside forces that inhibit us (Fisher in Jarow 2022). More importantly, we lose interest in protecting those institutions that preserve liberal universalist principles like liberal democracy and human rights, because we no longer see them as the thing that frees us (Fisher 2022 in Jarow).

We are not obligated to abide by the algorithm's choices. One could argue that algorithms simply provide a *nudge* that alters users behaviour without forbidding any options (Thaler and Sunstein 2008). Just because YouTube auto-plays the next video, I am under no obligation to watch it. Central to the *algorithmic contract* is the fact that we can opt-out but seldom choose to. If the algorithm eliminated your choices, then users would perceive this as a form of coercion. Algorithms do not force us to choose options against our will. We have agency. We can opt out of the platform. Yet, we often abide by the algorithm. As an example, 80 per cent of movies that people watch on Netflix come from the recommendation algorithm (Fisher in Jarow 2022).

The fact that alternatives outside of the recommendation algorithm are 'out there' for us to theoretically find is what keeps algorithmic recommendation from being a form of direct coercion. Our age is one of unprecedented access to a wide range of information, culture, and entertainment. We have never lived in an era that allowed for so many different expressions of what John Stuart Mill (2022, 57–76) called 'experiments in living'. Part of the algorithmic contract builds upon this classic utilitarian framework.

The Internet writ large offers an endless palate of 'experiments in living'. We, as autonomous Kantian 'ends in and of ourselves' (Kant 2017, 156–159), have the right to 'judge the good' for ourselves. We have the capacity (and the right) to order our preferences and determine the proper outcome. From a utilitarian perspective, this view of humanity benefits society by either showing others why received 'experiments' need to be modified or why our own personal 'experiments in living' must evolve to satisfy our needs.

Fisher (2020, 378–379) gives us a useful analogy to understand why this unlimited choice is coercive: he draws a distinction between 'the diary' and 'the ledger'. The ontology of the diary, he argues, is one which prioritizes writing. Through the 'technology' of writing, we get reflection upon the self. Without reflecting upon our experiments in living we fail to develop a greater awareness of ourselves. The ontology of the diary is the enlightenment of human seeking self-knowledge. The ledger, by contrast, is the 'technology' of record keeping. It just records empirical observations and focuses more on quantification of the self rather than individual critical awareness through a hermeneutic. The ontology of the ledger is the ontology of the algorithm. Fisher described the distinction as follows during a 2022 interview:

> [I]magine a reality where each individual is represented by a personal ledger where all digital footprint is registered, accumulated, sorted, and rendered into knowledge about the self through mathematical and technological devices: algorithms, machine learning, artificial intelligence, and so forth. ... The diary assumed a subject which becomes aware of itself, and a media through which subjectivity could be developed. It facilitates critical knowledge, which involves reflexivity, and a struggle for subjectivity, striving to enlarge the realm of freedom. (Fisher in Jarow 2022)

Without the diary, we lack the time to reflect upon our online experiments in living. A fragmented, uncertain self with no time to reflect upon rapid changes can be psychologically destabilizing for many and does not cultivate the habits of good citizenship for society in general. Émile Durkheim's (1951) concept of 'anomie' accurately captures this condition. Anomie refers to a state of normlessness or lack of social regulation in society. Anomie occurs when rapid social changes take place, particularly during periods of industrialization or economic upheaval, weakening social cohesion and collective consciousness. In this state, individuals experience a disconnection from society due to unclear or ineffective social norms, values, and standards to guide behaviour. This breakdown in social regulation can lead to feelings of purposelessness, frustration, and despair among individuals, potentially resulting in increased rates of deviant behaviour, crime, and suicide. Despite the social ills it produces, anomie is what the algorithmic contract demands in return for the Library of Babel. In exchange for endless possibility, platforms demand near continuous engagement for the purpose of data collection and reflection is not compatible with online engagement. This continuous engagement is necessary to order and classify users into valid market clusters.

Ordinalization in the algorithmic contract

Fisher argues that many of us are engaged in a process of 'ceding the toil of choice to the algorithm' (Fisher in Jarrow 2022). But what does this mean in practice? If the only thing the algorithmic contract did was remove the burden of choosing, that by itself would be inadequate to relieve anxiety. Beyond the choices presented to us by the algorithm, there remains a sea of possibility. Structuring our choices does not relieve the larger existential anxiety that our view of the world is wrong. Sartre's (2007, 29) belief that he was 'condemned to be free' still resonates regardless of the optimization algorithm. An additional element of the algorithmic contract that relieves users' anxiety is *ordinalization*. By shaping and solidifying our online identities through recommendation, the algorithm does not simply choose for us, it helps to instil a sense of meaning and identity for us. Algorithmic choosing is not simply a practice of 'giving users what they want', it is an exercise in shaping what users should want in the future. It is a practice of *editability*, rather than simply *legibility*.

The language of the social contract is useful for considering why we allow this algorithmic editability. Editability is akin to Walter Benjamin's (2008 [1935], 214–218) thinking on the development of the camera. By allowing users to reproduce images, the camera stripped the subject of a photo of its 'aura', its uniqueness in time and space. Before the camera, there was a sense of distance between the viewer and the work of art. One had to travel to a museum to see a great masterpiece. This gave artworks a 'presence' and authority that was grounded in religious and ritualistic experience. But the camera brought art closer to the viewer by allowing its reproduction, unmooring it from its temporal and spatial context. Benjamin thought that despite this removal of aura, the camera also democratized art and created possibilities for change).

In a very similar way, the algorithmic contract strips us as subjects of our aura by uprooting us from our physical contexts, making the fact of us and others as physical subjects less relevant. Parts of the algorithmic contract, like many social contracts that govern our lives, are ones that we do not necessarily agree to entirely. The adoption of the smartphone and the rise in engagement algorithms disrupted traditional structures of socialization. Before the Internet, socialization was rooted in place, driven by family socialization or local institutions. In the 20th century, technologies began to challenge the localized nature of cultural transmission, but even the radio, the TV, film, and other forms of mass culture experienced a 'friction' that reduced its spread. The TV and the radio were in a physical space. One had to go to the cinema to watch a movie. The internet tore local cultural transmission asunder, but what really accelerated the challenge to 'rooted socialization' was the engagement algorithm and the smartphone.

Fourcade and Healy (2024) argue that we live in an 'ordinal society' in which a growing share of what we do is captured, categorized, and scored on some algorithmic metric. At its root, ordinalization is a desire to discover, to find solutions, to improve or perfect simply for the pleasures of discovery. What was once driven by a DIY hacker impulse gave way to the discovery of how software firms could use the 'behavioral surplus' created by social media tools, to make shareholders profitable (Zuboff 2019). In the early days of social media, there was a serious question as to whether platforms could make a profit off users sharing vacation pictures. Facebook (Meta) was not always one of the largest companies in the world. For much of its rise, the question of 'monetization' loomed over it. In reasonably fast order, the commodification of consumer data became profitable as a means of advertising. As Fourcade and Healy (2024, 11) tell it, 'companies breathed in the exhaust fumes of their own data and found that it smelled of money'.

Before the widespread use of recommendation algorithms, sites relied on simpler strategies. In the 2000s, Google ranked pages based on how often a keyword appeared on the website (Gillespie 2014). The explosion in Google search use came with the advent of the personalization algorithm. Once Google could return searches based on your personal profile, it could improve the accuracy of search results. These early page rank algorithms posed a computational problem that was effectively addressed using personalized search histories. But there is a great deal of difference between improving search and collecting vast troves of individual data and using a machine learning model with thousands, if not millions, of parameters collected from you to predict future behaviour. The goal of the algorithm switched from enhancing your Google search results, to creating a better profile of you for the purposes of targeted advertising.

If the Google model is oriented around helping users find things online, users still have some form of agency and autonomy. However, models seeking to predict future behaviour, coupled with impressive advances in computational power, data storage, and data collection capacity, manufacture preferences instead of catering to them. In 2018, Google launched a feature called AutoAds that began using AI with its Adsense model to not only determine the content of ads but their placement. A beta test of AutoAds revealed 10 per cent greater engagement through this innovation (Srinivasan 2020).

This is not simply a process of helping you find products you might like. It is a process of finding ways to modify your behaviour so you can be guided towards what you should like. Much of the algorithmic age is an exercise in addressing the subject as an *algorithmic problem*. If the subject has a tendency to be too unpredictable, too capricious in their choices, then the algorithm is tasked to optimize their consumption. If data is the new oil (Toonders 2014), individuals that are unclassifiable and remain algorithmic problems are equivalent to a 'dry hole' for oil companies – a well that does not produce enough oil or gas. The task for social media companies, then, is to make subjects more predictable by imposing a classification scheme on them, something that can be both utterly predictable and deeply contingent. If 'algorithmic sorting' can also serve to relieve the anxiety of choosing, all the better.

Subjects as a commodity are only useful if they are consistent. If we remain algorithmic problems, then we are of little value to tech companies. We are 'free riding' off the tools that tech companies provide without cost. Unpredictable, idiosyncratic users provide no capacity for market segmentation. Idiosyncrasy (by definition) cannot scale, it cannot turn a profit, so the algorithms need to be turned on the users to habituate them toward something – anything – so long as it can be classified. This is where engagement algorithms are valuable – if there is a way to make users less serendipitous and more predictable, they become more valuable data commodities.

The algorithm as the basis of 'identity formation' has been slowly building for the last decade. Before social media and the algorithmic age, identity formation was a community-driven process, rooted in place, institution (family, religion, neighbourhood, school, and so on), and tradition. In 2017, Facebook adopted the slogan 'Bringing the World Closer Together' in its marketing materials and public statements. At the 2017 F8 developer conference, CEO Mark Zuckerberg expanded on the platform's new ambitious mission of creating a 'world community':

> For the last decade, we've focused on making the world more open and connected. But now we're at this point where we have to take that next step. We have to build a world where everyone has a sense of purpose and community. That's how we'll bring the world closer together. (Zuckerberg 2017)

Zuckerberg was unwittingly tapping into Adam Smith's classic idea of moral sentiments: that humans have a natural inner capacity for developing empathy (Smith 2010 [1759]). Through this empathy, we build community and can imagine ourselves in other's shoes. This allows us to develop a sense of shared fate through interaction with others. Community was hence central to the development of virtues like prudence, limiting harm, helping neighbours, and self-restraint.

The 'communities' that Facebook and other social media platforms are creating lack moral sentiments. The relationship between social media and negative outcomes is complex and potentially bi-directional, but over the last decade, numerous studies have linked social media to a number of negative social traits, like the increased risk of mental health problems, especially for adolescents who spend more than three hours a day on the platform (Khalaf et al 2023). Heavy social media users are more prone to sleep disruption (Levenson et al 2017). Social media users are exposed to idealized images and relentless self-comparison that often leads to negative body issues (Jiosta et al 2021). Teens are particularly vulnerable to cyberbullying and harassment on social media platforms (Garett et al 2016).

We have learned over the last decade that classification is not community. While democracies might be more aspirational, markets are more transactional. Rather than spend valuable time trying to figure out how to understand each other for the purposes of living in community, markets simply want to know how to meet individual needs. Meeting needs requires knowing something about the customers you want to serve. True community complicates the acquisition of this knowledge, or at least the organic community you find in the world. The natural pluralism of humans means they will learn from one another and evolve in their tastes, conditions, and values. This process of wanting to know about your neighbour's life, as you would in a healthy polis, comes with the corresponding possibility that you might change their mind and 'become unknowable' to the algorithm. Before social media, advertisers' understanding of individuals was crude and the tools they had at their disposal limited. Advertisers were left to rely on the logic of public opinion derived through inferential statistics or through focus groups. The need to create mass publics (hence the term mass marketing) was the only game in town.

The construction of identity groups has never been organic. Mora (2014) persuasively claims that the construction of the term 'Hispanic' was both a political and a socioeconomic construction designed to present fifty million individuals from nations of Spanish-speaking origin in the United States as speaking with one voice and having shared commercial tastes and political interests. From a marketing perspective, having this large group justified creating television networks like Univision and Telemundo that advertisers could use to access 'the Latino community'.

But the construction of an algorithmic community is something distinct. Engagement algorithms link individuals together through a shared set of aesthetic or ideological choices. Young people who might meet on platforms friendly to LGBTQ+ communities, like Tumblr, might also get similar music recommendations, or YouTube videos or Instagram 'shorts' recommendations. These communities are imagined. Anderson (1983) viewed nations as 'imagined political communities' who saw themselves as belonging together even if, in most cases, they had never met one another. Through print media, strangers could otherwise create a shared narrative that contributed to a sense of cultural rootedness and belonging rooted in nation, creed, or culture.

Recommendation algorithms create similar types of imagined communities, but through obscure algorithmic classification. In the pre-algorithmic era, mass marketing appeals were direct and transparent. Efforts to form group solidarity and community were promoted by themes and symbols that one could either embrace, reject, or be ambivalent towards. Recommendation algorithms are mysterious in ways that mass marketing is not. There are no signifiers pointing you towards your community membership. If you are 'in community' on Netflix over a shared taste in films, algorithms provide you no guidance regarding norms of behaviour or ethical guidelines regarding what it means to be in this community.

Algorithms turn us into 'ordinal citizens' (Fourcade and Healy 2024). Modern citizenship is shifting from a relationship between the individual and the state to one that is characterized by multiple, polycentric relationships between citizen and corporation, platform and non-profit entity (Fourcade and Healy 2024). This shift is not one of degree, but one in kind. Rather than citizenship based on the traditional liberal contract between citizen and state, ordinal citizenship is based on market transaction. Just like the social contract, the citizen cannot really opt out of this system of data collection and analysis. Even if you use no social media, you still have a large trove of online data about yourself that is used in the classification process. Ordinal citizenship is more transactional and rationalized, based more on a client/agent relationship than a set of civic loyalties (Fourcade and Healy 2024).

But, unlike traditional rights regimes, this current conception of ordinal citizenship is more blended and obscured. Fourcade (2021) uses finance as an example of a digitized space where the users are included in the financial system but their rights in this algorithmically obscure 'black box society' (Pasquale 2015) is hard to define. Obligation is placed on the user to manage their finances without a clear sense of how the algorithm will classify them. We are ranked without knowing the parameters used in our classification. Ordinal citizens have no civic life. This speaks to the paradox of the algorithmic contract – it both produces and promises to resolve the anxieties of our algorithmic age.

This ordinalization of social goods creates a redefinition of meritocracy. Rather than meritocracy being solely based on discernible effort and initiative, 'merit' is revealed through a vast network of data points, collected and analysed to rank subjects. This new slightly different form of meritocracy relies on having a granular knowledge about individuals, acquired through 'ordinal technologies' that take the vast amounts of data collected on each of us and creates a high dimensionality score (Fourcade and Healy 2024,

246–248). The data could contain location data, status updates, public records, tax data, Fitbit records, likes and follows on social media, web searches, credit scores, and countless other pieces of data that can be linked together to create a comprehensive profile of an individual. All of us then live in a digital surveillance state where decisions about our futures are shaped by this process of ordinalization. Through this process, one's experience of life is dictated by one's ordinality.

The implications for this ordinal citizenship go beyond simply structuring our choices or providing us with nudges to action. In the Lockean case, we leave the 'state of nature' and forfeit some of our natural sovereignty to a state in exchange for the protection of rights (Locke 1996 [1689]). In the United States, these rights are codified into the Constitution and Bill of Rights. These documents explicitly spell out the rights and liberties guaranteed by the state. In an ordinal society, however, what determines how those rights and liberties will be implemented is based on aggregated data that has been analysed and scored to create some type of optimization metric, without our full understanding or acquiescence.

These are not scores based on us as individuals but based on our algorithmically abstracted digital selves. This collection of data artifacts shapes the algorithmic truth about us – a truth that is distinctly different from our actual selves. As Koopman (2015) points out, '[w]e have … become subjects of our data, what I like to call "informational persons" who conceive of ourselves in terms of the status updates, check-ins, and other informational accoutrements we constantly assemble'. The hoard of data collected from us, by invitation via engagement algorithms, constitutes a datafied 'second self': a self that is 'from us' but not entirely constitutive 'of us' (Koopman 2015). Unsupervised machine learning classification models allow for the clustering of individuals into groups that individuals themselves may not even recognize themselves as members of. By allowing recommendation algorithms to 'choose for us' on social media platforms, companies learn enough about us to rank us and determine whether we are 'chosen' to receive resources and/or social rights.

The clustering has an iterative effect. If recommendation algorithms are purportedly 'giving you want you want' to encourage more engagement, you unwittingly reify to your own classification when you accept the algorithm's choice. Hence, the algorithmic contract has the paradoxical effect of seeming to give users agency and autonomy while accelerating the process of their ordinalization. This clustering does not challenge the individualistic notions of moral deservedness and social desirability. Ordinal citizenship is then actuarial rather than merit-based (Fourcade 2021). Actuarial logic is focused more on extracting value from user data for prediction and risk management than on determining merit (Fourcade and Healy 2017). This constitutes a darker side of the algorithmic contract, where our ceding of the *burden of choosing* to the algorithm becomes the basis of an algorithmic classification of risk.

Political power and the algorithmic contract

Central to the management of risk is the predictability of the subjects in question. But why do we agree to be algorithmically classified? The algorithmic contract not only classifies us, but provides us with the illusion of a new, more simplified self. In this way, the algorithmic contract and the social contract are similar – they both embody a sense of possibility. Hobbes (and Locke) take as axiomatic in the social contract the view that liberty constitutes 'freedom from' the absence of external restraint. According to Hobbes (1967 [1651]), you are free if no one is preventing you from acting. Even if you are acting from a position of ignorance or material lack, the social contract contends that you are still 'free' as you were in the 'state of nature'. If you do not have the power to act as you wish, you still have the freedom to seek out that power through your efforts and talents.

But the algorithmic contract differs in one key respect. Algorithms, by structuring your choice, are not restraining you per se; it can be argued that they are 'empowering you' by aiding you in becoming something different, perhaps better. By abstracting yourself, there is a possibility of finding a better you. Algorithms did not begin this process. Human history has been a process of cumulative learning where technological developments, like stone toolmaking, produced increased leisure time for humans (Barsky 2022). This leisure time unlocked innovation and paved the way for more complex societies. Without these technologies, there would have been no time for the development of language, myths, and symbols, leading to abstract thought.

This increase in abstraction, however, also creates a detachment from the natural world. These abstractions free us up to enjoy more leisure, but they also constrain us by changing our relationship with the world. We easily fall into the trap of seeing this as a 'simple/complex' dichotomy, when we can just as easily refer to it as 'flexible/rigid'. More nature-bound societies are more flexible because they have limited contact with data collection tools. By relieving us from the burden of choosing, algorithms curate our information and entertainment diets in unprecedented ways. Algorithms abstract us in ways that previous technologies could not. In the algorithmic contract, we implicitly trust that the algorithm will serve our needs. It will entertain us or inform us about the world 'out there'. Students of behavioural psychology know that the amygdala does not always steer us towards that which serves our objective needs. We can be fooled into thinking that our algorithmically steered choices are made freely and autonomously. If we are becoming abstracted, classified selves, who benefits? How do we change the algorithmic contract?

Technology companies have significant power in the United States. This is evident in the dominance of American tech company founders and CEOs on the global list of wealthiest individuals. Figures like Jeff Bezos, Elon Musk, and Mark Zuckerberg exemplify the concentration of wealth and power within this system, showcasing the United States as both a driver and a beneficiary of global capitalism. Accordingly, the tech sector's lobbying influence in Washington, DC has grown significantly in recent years, with profound implications for policy and regulation. A 2024 report by the global real estate services company JLL found that tech companies spent $342.1 million on lobbying efforts in 2023, a 40 per cent increase from 2020 (Technical.ly 2024). This surge in spending has been accompanied by a physical presence, with major tech firms establishing offices in Washington, DC and in state capitals to advocate for lenient algorithmic and AI safety regulations, successfully influencing key lawmakers. Major social media platforms collectively spent $30 million on lobbying in 2023, employing one lobbyist for roughly every four members of Congress (Combs 2024). A study by Public Citizen (Chen and Tanglis 2024) found 1,100 registered lobbyists focusing on AI-related issues in 2023 alone. Li (2023) found that tech lobbyists significantly influence the nature of digital trade policy discussions in Washington, DC, effectively positioning tech growth as central to national defence and economic growth.

Li (2023) argues that, in the context of technology, the regulatory capture in the United States is best explained by the technical nature of the issue. Lacking expertise, lawmakers often rely on industry insiders to help shape the regulatory agenda. This produces a 'revolving door', where regulators move in and out of the industry such that they become the regulated and vice versa. It is difficult for ordinal citizens to gain access to decision-making power. Advocacy groups would have to raise awareness of the negative impacts of algorithmic classification to mobilize everyday citizens. As E.E. Schattschneider (1960, 71) noted, 'all forms of political organization have a bias in favor of the exploitation of some kinds of conflict and the suppression of others because organization is the mobilization of bias. Some issues are organized into politics while others are organized out'. The algorithmic contract is a 'mobilization of bias' towards algorithmic classification. Most users are not software engineers that can determine how algorithms are deployed. There is growing awareness of the impact of algorithms among the mass public in recent years through popular culture documentaries like *The Social Dilemma*, blockbuster reports like the *Facebook Papers*, and high-profile lawsuits against tech companies (and their algorithms) for contributing to teen suicides (Cummins 2022; Murphy Kelly 2022).

Despite the intense scrutiny levelled at social media platforms, there are very few calls for the elimination, or even serious regulation, of algorithms in the United States. The belief that we control the algorithm, not vice versa, is a core element of the algorithmic contract. We believe this because engagement algorithms do not keep conflicts out of the public eye. If your politics lean far to the left or the right, you will not be denied access to opposing content, you will be fed a steady diet of it. This is central to the algorithmic contract. If you want to populate your feed with content that contests private power, the algorithm will gladly provide it to you. Those in power might actively work to prevent certain issues from gaining public attention, but the engagement algorithm does not appear to *have a politics* in that specific sense.

Algorithms have an *affective* politics. Algorithms steer users towards that which creates high-valence emotional responses. It constitutes a form of personalized agenda setting. By populating feeds with content that is emotionally and psychologically satisfying or enraging to the user, the algorithmic contract creates a sleight of hand. Rather than framing policy issues through agenda control, it creates the perception that the agenda is the whole, the abstraction is reality. There is no interest among most people in expanding the scope of conflict because we are algorithmically inundated with emotional conflict. This automatically diverts our attention away from policy issues requiring complexity, nuance, and sustained engagement.

Elites need not concern themselves with activists 'expanding the scope of conflict' because citizens' attention spans and cognitive bandwidths are so saturated that there is not room for policy issues to break through and make it onto the legislative agenda. To the extent that we do care about policy, algorithmic classification has produced in us ideological footings that make any effort at 'expanding the scope of conflict' a massive undertaking. This constructed polarization, in and of itself, offers a sort of stability to elite decision makers who can be assured that the mass public will be either too distracted, or too solidified, in their political identity to be mobilized for meaningful political action. Certainly, users will be mobilized. The mass protests around the killing of George Floyd in Minneapolis in 2020 were an indication of the capacity and willingness of people to engage in mass action, but the policy response was muted because of an anaemic legislative response in the United States – a response that results from the calcification of political identities. If individuals are living abstracted political identities because of their algorithmically curated lives, there is little room for mass protest to 'expand the scope of conflict' by winning adherents to their cause. In the case of Black Lives Matter protests, the rigidity of our classified politics means there were few 'converts' to the cause and little need for legislative response.

This makes our politics *predictable*. Elites can be confident that the public has detached from policy expectations. Instead of focusing on significant political matters, those who engage in politics on social media are often engaging in either extolling their position or mocking those with whom they disagree. The rest assiduously avoid the messiness of politics, lest they get caught up in the nasty business of policing identity boundaries (elevating exemplars or identifying transgressors and ridiculing them). But those who do not partake in politics leave the field open to the 'chronically online', which creates the sense that all politics is an exercise in boundary maintenance. This ensures that politics becomes a neoliberal spectacle, not unlike the lifestyle aestheticism discussed in previous chapters.

Algorithmic structuration

This politics of predictability has its virtues. An affective politics that encourages the formation of orthodoxies does not predetermine which orthodoxy you select, and it does not by definition preclude a critique of capitalism or democracy. It does, however, demand orthodoxy. Our acquiescence to the algorithmic contract is driven more by the incentive to 'fit the model', to move at one's own 'learning rate' toward the 'local minima' of one's given classification. This movement does not need to have a 'man behind the curtain' driving it. It is a form of algorithmic 'structuration'. Structuration is the reproduction of social structures – understandings and meanings. It proceeds intergenerationally through norms and habits without any intentional act (Giddens 1999). To illustrate structuration, Hayward (2009) uses the example of a woman learning the Argentine Tango. To do the dance, she responds to the male dancer who always leads. These moves reproduce the constitution of a woman's relative powerlessness without any actor or agent declaring it to be so (Hayward 2009, 181).

The algorithm serves a similar function. Once ensnared into the world of data production and collection, we are subject to the laws of the 'dance'. Algorithmic classification is not solely abstracting the self from nature but is modifying the nature of the self in novel ways. We develop online identities/brands and build online communities that reinforce those identities/brands. Algorithmic recommendation amplifies the ideologies and aesthetics of those communities. Deviating from these communities presents challenges for us – we might get ostracized or ignored. We have the autonomy to decide which 'dance' we want to learn, but once we have chosen, we are subject to its laws.

In Prague, there is a statue of the writer Franz Kafka by Czech sculptor Jaroslav Róna, titled *The Empty Suit*. The statue has a man riding atop a giant empty suit as if it were a horse. Huenemann (2021) interprets the statue's meaning: 'A man rides an empty suit. The suit tells others what to think of the man … The man does not control the suit, but merely takes a ride upon it, come what may.' The 'man riding a suit' is a useful metaphor for thinking about the power in the algorithmic contract. Classification algorithms are very much like a suit you are given to wear – a specific, abstracted way of seeing the world. A different suit would take the rider on a different path.

The algorithmic contract gives us the promise of 'riding a new suit'. We can build an identity online that is separate and distinct from our offline selves. This suit gives us an ability to act differently than we otherwise would. It is a constitutive power, meaning our power depends on our 'role' in a given situation (Foucault 1976). It is a 'technology of the self' that can exert a positive (or at least agentic) influence on life, 'striving to administer, optimize, and multiply its influence while subjecting it to precise controls and comprehensive regulations' (Foucault 1976, 137). Where the algorithm differs is in the fact that there is no agent controlling or regulating behaviour. It is a 'power to' rather than 'power over' (Arendt 1972, 140). It is an alluring power of being in a virtual community of like-minded others. As humans, our core means of expressing power is through public, collective action, or as Arendt (1972, 44) put it, the 'ability to act in concert' to enact change.

This was the empowering Internet of 2012: of brave Iranians and Tunisians risking their lives to tweet out the location of the next protest rally. If social media is prismatic, at one time the prism produced a beautiful rainbow of colours (Bail 2021). People wore 'suits' that prompted collective action. This version of the web reminds us that abstraction/classification can be both empowering and constraining. From a biopolitics perspective, technology normalizes power by giving us the tools to 'self-regulate' to fit a current knowledge regime. Any of us with Fitbits and ten pounds we think we need to lose knows the hold that self-regulation has on us. We can think of categorization, not as intrusive state 'legibility' but as a tool of empowerment. The possibility of an empowering classification is what makes the algorithmic contract appealing to users – the possibility of a more empowered self through classification/group membership.

The algorithmic contract and automated control

But in an appropriately Kafkaesque way, the suits are both illusory and all-encompassing. Illusory in that they are abstractions of reality. All-encompassing in that, in their clarity and certitude, they can appear to be 'more real' than reality itself. Algorithmic curation creates an ontological certitude about the world that goes beyond simply 'playing a role' or 'wearing a suit'. Massumi (2015) uses the term 'ontopower' to refer to power operating at the level of being itself, shaping the environment and the conditions of life in an ambient, pervasive manner. In the algorithmic contract, we welcome classification and ordinalization because it encourages us to adopt a tidier, more certain view of the world. But this classification becomes our ontology. We see the world through the lens of our cluster, which encourages dualistic thinking (in-group versus out-group). Rather than viewing this constitutive power as solely empowering, an ontopower approach helps us understand how it can also be destructive.

Ontopower switches the emphasis of state and society from 'deterrence' to 'preemption' (Massumi 2015). Deterrence is based on the idea that threats can be identified, understood, and managed by identifying the threat and broadcasting consequences to deter unwanted actions. It relies on an empirical understanding of threats – assuming that it is possible to know where threats are coming from and why they exist. More importantly, it assumes the threat is an agent whose behaviour can be changed, either through reason or sanction. It posits an agent whose mind can be changed.

Algorithms operate on the principle of pre-emption, which seeks to neutralize threats before they materialize. Pre-emption does not require the need for understanding motivations or even identifying them clearly. Pre-emption does not prioritize communicating with or working with potential threats to reduce them, but rather it focuses on structuring the environment in such a way that threats are eliminated before they can cause any damage. The subject of the threat in this case is not an independent agent with rights or a fellow citizen whose actions can be modified. The subject is an 'outlier' whose existence we do not need to understand. We do not need to get to the root causes of aberrant behaviour. We prefer it to be eliminated or ushered out of view.

A preference for pre-emption over deterrence is a core element of the algorithmic contract. This can only be possible if users begin to adopt an abstracted view of themselves through algorithmic engagement. They begin to see themselves and others as classified abstractions rather than complex human beings. Increasing support for cruel and barbaric treatment of immigrants in the United States and Europe serve as examples of populations who have been algorithmically trained to see the other as an abstraction, not a human subject with a rich inner life.

Algorithms influence and manage the emotional lives of citizens. They are a form of ontopower in that they are able to control users' sense of themselves, their prospects, and their reaction to their life circumstances through subtle, often invisible, means (Massumi 2015). In the 2024 US presidential election, supporters for both sides became convinced their candidate was going to win because the algorithmically mediated environment in which each lived was guided by ontopower. Supporters of both candidates were fed a steady diet of social media posts through which they became convinced of their candidate's certain victory and which worked to invalidate any counter-information they received.

Pre-emption works by altering the environment and the conditions under which decisions are made, thus guiding outcomes in a way that minimizes the emergence of threats altogether. Abstraction gives us the perception of control and safety. An abstracted self is a less complex, more comprehensible self. A world full of abstracted selves are more easily dealt with in ways that present fewer emotional and ethical challenges for citizens. We ourselves live in environments that pre-empt other possibilities, and that in turn makes it easier for us to advocate for pre-emption strategies to eliminate threats to our abstracted, algorithmically mediated environment. The elimination of these threats often does not serve the interests of users, but of elites. We accept a pre-emption view for a number of reasons: the lack of a political consensus on deterrence strategies, the belief in a 'dismal view' of human nature that presumes 'undisciplinable subjects', and the lure of 'technosolutionism' (Andrejevic 2019). But the algorithmic contract exacerbates this desire for pre-emption over deterrence. In this instance, power ceases to be *empowering*, simply another form of control. This restricts the possibilities of identity play – of 'trying on different suits', or reflecting on whether one wants to try a different suit.

The search for meaning and identity becomes replaced under the algorithmic contract with a desire to pre-empt ourselves – to minimize our exposure to that which might challenge our 'suit' in favour of content that reinforces our algorithmically abstracted identities (in other words, that move towards the local minima). This process is reflexive, done with little forethought or analysis. The signal-to-noise ratio concept in cybernetic theory presumes that algorithms that can 'filter out noise' can more readily detect patterns (Shannon 1948). The 'noise' in this case is data and information that does not comport with our algorithmically induced identity. While the algorithm curates much of this noise for us, we become habituated towards the signal, only wanting information that reinforces our worldview or allows us to performatively mock or discredit contrary information.

When applied to human thought and behaviour, this drive towards optimizing the signal by eliminating the noise is a 'derangement of rationality' (Halpern 2015, 146–151). Optimizing the signal is different than reason, which focuses on the cultivation of values that lead to human flourishing. Rationality is the practice of value-free optimization, regardless of the goal. In the world of algorithms, nuance is equated with noise. This parallels how people with algorithmically abstracted ideological worldviews are more easily categorized, as their predictable nature makes them less noisy.

Social media platforms, whether by accident or design, tend to favour and amplify strong moral claims. Such claims not only attract attention and engagement but also provoke similarly strong responses. While we understand this dynamic in terms of engagement algorithms, it also serves to reduce noise within the model, simplifying the classification of user behaviour. People are unpredictable, with needs that make them 'sub-optimal' workers and citizens. One of the promises of AI for companies is the belief that it can replace knowledge workers across a range of fields, therefore increasing efficiency and profitability. This logic also applies to nation states that hope that ambient surveillance and anomaly detection can replace much of the work of human intelligence gathering and analysis. If we can make subjects more predictable, that lessens the risk for market and state actors that subjects will behave in sub-optimal (that is, human) ways.

This is not the way algorithms are sold to us. They are sold as tools that will aid our human flourishing. Tech companies advocate for 'humans in the loop' accountability structures. We rightly believe that, even if algorithms can sort and compute better than we can, they do not have the problem-solving capability of humans. We, after all, have the capacity to adapt our thinking to changing circumstances (Floridi 2023). Algorithms may be able to optimize, but they do not have the capability of classical reasoning, or the wisdom to make value judgements. The example that comes to mind for me is my inability to beat my AI chess app. This app is optimized for the task of being proficient at chess, but that same algorithm (Stockfish) could not then turn around and recommend films for me to watch. This, however, is changing rapidly. An emerging technique, 'digital twinning', allows for the creation of a digital copy of a hardware object (a robot, for example) and through deep learning neural networks, the copy can be trained through 'reinforcement learning' to do a new task and placed back into the hardware to apply this learning to the new environment. This allows for machines to adopt some of the adaptability characteristics we once thought were reserved for humans.

We are quickly moving from an analogue, human-driven, mechanized world to an automated prediction-based one (Grove 2019). Machines are adopting human-like characteristics, allowing them to adapt to diverse circumstances. Applied to economic productivity or health care, these characteristics could be beneficial to humanity, but applied to war they become 'cunning machines' capable of killing with autonomy and precision (Grove 2020, 437). As we move towards a society more characterized by prediction and automation, this produces unanticipated consequences for human agency and collective action. A public comfortable with pre-emption is one that fails to mobilize to challenge unlawful uses of power. Citizens that have algorithmically curated information diets are ontologically shielded from the worst abuses of power. Elites can more readily exploit people and resources through technological automation without significant or effective outcry. The personal toll of warfare is reduced by the automation of war, allowing nation states to pursue extraterritorial violence without facing the repercussions from their populations (Grove 2019).

The increased automation of society produces a 'dark enlightenment' movement that advocates for the abolition of democracy to be replaced by a techno-corporate dictatorship (Grove 2019). This movement rejects the ideas of the liberal enlightenment, presuming that humans are not equal and that a 'meritocratic' elite should govern society, with the rest of the disposable populations either marginalized or managed through technological manipulation. This shift towards a dark enlightenment can only happen through the acquiescence of the public who sees in algorithmic categorization and abstraction the possibility of a new self. The spillover effects of abstracting ourselves is that we abstract others, making it more likely to see them as 'dangerous others'. We observe this in the anti-immigrant and nationalist politics gaining strength in liberal democracies around the world. The algorithmic contract's promise of a 'new identity' through classification and abstraction changes our goals from seeing integration and commonality towards optimizing towards the group membership (local minima).

Citizens succumb to an 'algocracy' where humans increasingly accept automated decision-making in their lives (Aradau and Blanke 2022, 288). Everything becomes an optimization task, extending optimization principles to all areas of life. This 'optimization of everything' collapses to the 'epistemic tension between the large and the small' (Aradau and Blanke 2022, 31). Through the ability to 'datafy everything' where the 'N' represents both the sample size and the totality of the data, algorithms are able to blend the global and the particular in ways that impact both. Algorithms allow for a complex 'decomposition' and 'recomposition' of the self: 'Algorithmic reason conjoins *omnes et singulatim*, the particular and the general, the part and whole, the individual and the population. Its distinctive promise is not that of endless correlation or infinite association, but that of surmounting the epistemic separation of large-N/small-n through relations that are endlessly decomposable and recomposable' (Aradau and Blanke 2022, 35).

This allows those in power to produce human–machine assemblages of populations 'recomposed' in the service of a client, be it the military seeking to enhance security or a corporation looking to increase profit. The challenge in the age of algorithmic reason is how to evaluate truth claims offered by different 'data recompositions'. The algorithmic contract constitutes an agreement where we adhere to being 'decomposed' and 'recomposed' in ways that relieve the anxiety, boredom, banality, or complexity of our real-world human existence and optimizes our environment so that we are ontologically blinded from the 'noise' of alternative viewpoints.

This has dire consequences for liberal democracy. Liberal democracies are messy. It is difficult to build consensus because liberalism is individualistic and heterogeneous. With its emphasis on preserving the rights of individuals, liberalism wants to protect rights and resolve conflict through reason and dialogue. The emphasis on liberal democracy is to seek agreement through dialogue and compromise. The risk in liberal democracies is that the desire to ensure that every voice is heard can slow down or gridlock the process of enacting necessary changes. A culture that increasingly demands 'optimization in everything' may see liberalism as feckless and incapable of action.

Remaining an algorithmic problem

A world in which all algorithmically mediated identities are optimized is one where deliberation and consensus is impossible. At best we can arrive at an 'agree to disagree' posture where conflict and contestation is a given and liberal democracy is characterized by 'undecidability … [where a] final emancipation is neither possible, nor desirable', a condition that leaves us in a continual state of disagreement (Laclau and Mouffe 2014, 10–19). But the ability to deconstruct and reconstruct identities and narratives does not take place on an even playing field. We are engaged in asymmetrical warfare with the owners of data and algorithms. They get to decompose and recompose us to suit their projects. 'Sousveillance' strategies (watching the watcher) as a means to 'level the playing field' do not work in an era where elites have significant computation advantages over the masses (Mann 2009). The velocity, variety, and volume of data and the opaque nature of algorithms and their outputs make it difficult to envision a reasonable sousveillance regime being practicable today.

Ideally, the algorithmic contract would promote civic life and democratic health. Liberal democracy is as concerned with legitimacy and accountability as it is with outputs. Citizens should have a right to shape the ways in which these tools are used, not to improve optimization, but as a value in and of itself (Simons 2023). We cannot remove algorithms from decision-making, but we can think through how they can combine with humans to produce better outcomes. A first step in this process is to renegotiate the algorithmic contract such that users become algorithmic problems.

It is not an obvious question as to why a society needs citizens that become algorithmic problems. You can make a reasonable case that the goal of any social order should be to reduce the amount of dissent that exists. Too much idiosyncrasy makes liberal democracy unwieldy and difficult to govern. American political scientists in the 1950s thought the aggregation of interests should be a priority for liberal democratic societies. David Truman (1951), in *The Governmental Process*, contended that interest groups serve as an essential link between citizens and government, aggregating and articulating diverse societal interests. From this vantage point, competition is a cornerstone of pluralist democracy, ensuring that multiple perspectives are represented in policy making (Dahl 1961). Defenders argue that this system allows specialized knowledge and broader representation of all stakeholders involved in policy.

Becoming an algorithmic problem does not mean the fostering of a society of idiosyncratic contrarians that have conspiratorial or dangerous views. A liberal conception of autonomy as personal idiosyncrasy can conflict with democratic ideals of interdependence, collective decision-making and democratic citizenship (Pateman 1975; Nedelsky 1989).

But individuals who challenge official orthodoxies – artists, inventors, revolutionaries – are vital to social progress in liberal democracies. These types of outliers often push against established norms, inspiring new ways of thinking and acting. By challenging what is accepted, they not only innovate but also resist the staleness that can come from unquestioning obedience to authority when unmerited. In modern society, we do not lack people who question orthodoxies or disrupt existing frameworks. What we lack, instead, is a civil society where we can evaluate the legitimacy of such challenges. As society becomes more polarized and fragmented, the ability to engage in meaningful, collective debate over these challenges has diminished. One of the significant losses in this process is the breakdown of a shared language for discussing and evaluating questions of truth, reality, and knowledge – what might be called our 'ontological' and 'epistemological' realities. The problem is not the outlier, but the inability to vet the outlier's claims in ways that are seen as legitimate by the political community.

In earlier times, there was a clearer sense of what constituted a common civic discourse, a space where different viewpoints could be debated and resolved. Today, however, we have lost that shared framework, and, with it, the foundations of civic community. Without a common language for debate, society finds itself adrift, with no shared method of reconciling disagreements, whether they be about politics, science, or culture. This, in turn, reduces the willingness of individuals to be authentic outliers – to challenge the orthodoxy of their 'tribe' and run the risk of public shaming to uphold their idiosyncratic beliefs.

This fragmentation creates a legitimacy structure for those tech industry elites who view democracy as an inefficient or inadequate form of governance. As technology becomes more enmeshed in everyday life, tech elites may prioritize efficiency and innovation over democratic values such as legitimacy and representativeness. PayPal founder Peter Thiel recently noted his belief that 'freedom and democracy are incompatible' (Gellman 2023), noting that liberalism was 'weary' and expressing admiration for elite oligarchy as being more capable of achieving big things.). This belief in oligarchy as more efficient than the slower, messier processes of democratic governance is not restricted to isolated tech entrepreneurs.

Balaji Srinivasan, the chief technology officer of Coinbase, believes tech entrepreneurs should 'secede from democracy', in a manner reminiscent of the plot from the Ayn Rand novel *Atlas Shrugged* (Duran 2024). Srinivasan envisions tech-governed cities where supporters of the tech elites wear grey t-shirts and ally with police to identify dissenters (Duran 2024). While these ideas might seem far-fetched, democracy, with its inherent inefficiencies, can be vulnerable to technocratic elites that offer to use algorithmic optimization as the basis for a new, more orderly society.

Outliers, in this scenario, are critically needed to challenge the creeping ordinalization and optimization of society. Outliers offer viable counter-narratives to dominant ideologies, by presenting alternative ways of viewing the world, adding plurality to civic life, a core principle in liberal and deliberate models of democracy. Outlier voices challenge dominant narratives, encouraging debate and the critical examination of ideas. They serve as the basis for liberal society, the willingness to offer one's worldview to a broader audience ('conjecture') and the openness to have those ideas potentially proven wrong ('refutation') (Popper 1963). Acceptance of outliers fosters an environment where conjecture and refutation are valued, aligning with the deliberative democratic process, where public reasoning and argumentation are essential. Outliers push against consensus, forcing the broader public to reconsider assumptions and re-examine policies from different angles. By introducing new perspectives, they help to prevent the stagnation of civic discourse and contribute to a more dynamic, open society. Their presence ensures that multiple viewpoints are represented, which is crucial for the health of a liberal democracy. They serve as crucial figures for contesting the 'fencing in' of thought and action, preventing any one framework from becoming too rigid or ideological. This diversity of voices is essential to keeping a democracy dynamic and adaptable, ensuring that it remains a space for ongoing negotiation rather than settling into a fixed and unchallengeable order.

Mill's (2002 [1859]) classic utilitarian defence of free speech made room for outliers. If an outlier's idea is correct, it would eventually become accepted as truth. Conversely, if the idea is wrong, it serves to reinforce the validity of the existing orthodoxy. In this way, outliers play a vital role in the dynamic process of truth-seeking within society. Outliers, by questioning mainstream ideas, create space for alternative solutions to emerge, allowing society to adapt to new challenges. Outliers from marginalized groups or alternative ideologies bring fresh insights and alternative ways of understanding the world, offering counter-narratives that challenge the status quo. These counter-narratives are essential for maintaining a culture that is open to change and responsive to the needs of all its members. Political discourse, especially in liberal democracies, thrives on conversations that probe and challenge the status quo. Rarely does a single discussion change minds, but through the exchange of stories, narratives, and frames, people may begin to see the world differently. Democracy, therefore, requires a certain level of ambiguity – a 'fuzziness' that allows for having convictions, not rigid ideologies.

Even in democratic frameworks that are sceptical of consensus-seeking around truth claims, outliers serve as necessary grounds for contestation, actively resisting the 'fencing in' of thought and action by dominant forces. Agonistic theories of democracy view conflict and disagreement as inherent to the political process (Mouffe 2005). Rather than aiming for consensus, agonism values the expression of opposing views as a necessary aspect of democratic life. Outliers, by refusing to conform to the prevailing consensus, ensure that political spaces remain sites of active contestation. They resist the pressures to conform, providing grounds for continual renegotiation of power structures and social norms. This resistance is crucial in preventing any single ideology or framework from becoming too dominant, ensuring that democracy remains a space for ongoing political struggle rather than passive agreement.

Engagement algorithms are doing the opposite: they are curating the digital world to provide us with material that reinforces our worldview. When we are presented with 'experiments in living' that do not comport with our own, they are often presented as bizarre or grotesque. One might imagine someone who believes homosexuality is a sin is likely to have a social media feed that reinforces negative stereotypes of LGBTQ+ people.

It turns out individuals dislike change, that identity is not easily challenged, and that individuals like to be confirmed in the rectitude of their world views. We all possess a part of us that seeks moral clarity. Social media has empowered this aspect of our character by providing a platform for activism. However, the nature of social media often rewards moral clarity over reasonableness. Academics, for example, are trained to consider multiple perspectives and to entertain the possibility of being wrong, a mindset that is often at odds with the performative nature of online activism.

This tension between deliberate, inefficient inquiry and fast, certain optimization is the core challenge of our algorithmically driven society. Machine learning, with its focus on optimization, views doubt, contingency, and uncertainty as noise to be minimized. Social media engagement algorithms, in turn, reward posts that take strong moral, emotionally laden positions, rather than those that foster thoughtful inquiry. Posts that spread lies forcefully are favoured by engagement algorithms over posts that ask questions and invite conjecture and refutation. This creates a feedback loop where the desire for engagement leads to the promotion of easily classifiable posts, which then calcify our 'brands', which encourages us to adopt even stronger moral positions. The result is a political and aesthetic environment that favours certitude over conjecture, elevating ideologues while marginalizing good-faith inquiry. This shift has paradoxical consequences. On the one hand, algorithms have incentivized the dual role of individuals as both cultural consumers and producers. On the other hand, the relentless pursuit of optimization threatens to render human agency obsolete, reducing individuals to data points in a system that values predictability over complexity.

In this algorithmic age, where individualism and market rationalism are paramount, we see the erosion of collective values. The Internet, once heralded as a boon for democracy, has become clouded by bad faith actors and market imperatives. The segmentation of individualism, fuelled by algorithms, has led to a form of liberalism that prioritizes personal identity and market participation over community and equality. This has profound implications for civil society. The phenomenon of 'quiet quitting' in political discourse, where many people disengage from contentious discussions, is one symptom of a broader social recession. The most problematic mis/disinformation comes from a miniscule segment of the online population. Lazer et al (2018) found that 'only 1 percent of individuals accounted for 80 percent of fake news source exposures, and 0.1% accounted for nearly 80 percent of fake news sources shared'.

In the face of these changes, the challenge is not just to understand how algorithms shape our lives but to reclaim the aspects of our humanity that resist classification. This may involve embracing uncertainty, fostering creativity, and cultivating spaces where ambiguity and complexity are valued rather than suppressed. Ultimately, the algorithmic age represents a profound shift in how we understand ourselves and our place in the world. As we navigate this new landscape, the question remains: how can we maintain our humanity in a world increasingly governed by the logic of optimization, especially when market forces seek the predictability of the algorithmic contract? I turn to the ways in which technocapitalism reinforces the algorithmic contract in the next chapter.

5

The Classification Economy

When British Prime Minister Margaret Thatcher opined in an interview response to a question about public good provision that 'There is no such thing!' as government and that 'people [should] look to themselves first', she was reflecting the mood of the 1980s (Thatcher 1987). By the end of the 20th century, the view that liberal democracies had become too reliant on public sector social engineering to address social ills and that we needed to return to free-market individualism was becoming dominant. This thinking was rooted in the assumptions of the Austrian economists, a school of thinkers whose historical roots date back to the late scholastics of the 15th century who sought to justify the morality of commerce and profit-making (Rothbard 1998; Mises 1963; Hayek 1944). This group of economists diverged in some areas but held consistent beliefs about the efficiency and justness of markets, the prioritization of the individual over the collective, the virtue of market competition, and the importance of a minimal state. However, in an age of algorithmic optimization, where people's preferences are subtly influenced and shaped, do their assumptions still hold (if they ever did)? Do algorithms undermine the free market's reliance on independent judgement?

Key to understanding Austrian economists is the concept of *subjective value*. Because individuals differ in their tastes and preferences (and goods differ in their availability and utility to the individual), the value of goods lies within individuals – not inherently in goods themselves. This subjective value is reflected in human action – if I buy something, it means I value it more highly than the money I am paying for it, a concept referred to as 'Pareto optimality' (Henderson, nd).

Accordingly, if I am to arrive at a subjective assessment of the value of a good, I have to have some freedom and autonomy to determine for myself what I value. The view of classical economists requires a subject free from coercion, choosing based on the simple utility calculus that people act in ways that minimize costs and maximize benefits. This view has always been problematic. The 'choosing agent' has never existed independent of society. 'Utility-maximization' (optimization) is not a goal unto itself. It 'does not tell you where to go, but only that you should arrive there (or go part of the way) with the least effort' (Wildavsky in Stone 1988, 133).

In a world dominated by algorithms that curate choice, preferences are shaped by unseen forces, raising concerns about whether these 'subjective' choices are truly autonomous. Curation does not simply include which products are presented to the user, it also impacts the ways in which products are presented to users. The manner of presentation, time when the product is displayed on the platform, and cost the consumer sees for the product are all dictated algorithmically. Platforms employ algorithmic optimization towards prices. Lyft and Uber use their massive data repositories of traffic patterns to adopt 'surge pricing' to predict both the supply of drivers and the demand for rides given past patterns (Chen et al 2016). A number of industries have been using algorithmic optimization (airlines, hotels, and so on) to optimize the maximum price a specific user will pay for a service. Amazon uses its data to adjust the prices users see on its website based on factors like changes in competitor pricing, real-time inventory levels, and user behaviour (Chen et al 2016). Increasingly industries are employing AI to better personalize pricing strategies and marketing appeals to individual consumers. Britain's largest pub group, Stonegate, has experimented with surge pricing, charging 20 pence more per pint during peak hours (Al-Khalaf 2023).

The algorithmic contract relies on curation remaining in the background. Under the algorithmic contract, choice precedes preference, rather than the other way around. Recommendation algorithms present you with choices derived from your prior preferences, but they are also derived from 'others like you'. Yet they are presented as if they were derived from an atomized choosing agent. The collective involved in structuring your choice and the local minima which you are being steered towards is not visible. When watching YouTube, for instance, the recommendation algorithm presents some options but leaves out others. This algorithm reduces the range of infinite choices to a select few. The real 'independent agent' would engage in 'full information searches' to maximize utility. In reality, none of us do this. We use 'bounded rationality' to make decisions within the constraints of our cognitive limits and available time (Simon 1987, 25). The result is a process of 'satisficing' or finding a sub-optimal but satisfactory solution (Simon 1987, 295–298). In the algorithmic contract, we allow the algorithm to engage in a form of satisficing, presuming that it knows what our goals are based on our past behaviour.

Each time we sit down in front of YouTube, we are not starting anew, we are 'muddling through' (Lindblom 1959). The term applies to how government agencies in the United States navigate having to make policy decisions under social and political constraints. Government agencies do not reinvent the wheel when addressing policy problems because of the political costs inherent in breaking from convention, instead making incremental adjustments to existing policy. An agency head who breaks too far from what has been done in the past puts themselves at risk of suffering politically if things do not go as planned. Critics of government action point to this as a reason why the state finds it difficult to innovate. Similarly, the algorithm is like the government agency, encouraging us to muddle through content given to us by the recommendation engine. This serves two purposes: it makes users less likely to disengage from the platform and it makes users more predictable by encouraging them not the be too adventuresome in their 'search' for content. This is a useful way to think about how we become classified. Just like the learning rate hyperparameter dictates the speed at which we approach the local minima, we muddle through (or are muddled through) in a stepwise process towards our prescribed categories.

Algorithms sort, classify, and seek patterns in structure. Any effort at classification inevitably highlights certain aspects of the classified object while diminishing others. This is a liability that researchers accept for the sake of lending insight into social phenomena. However, with algorithmic classification as it is currently applied, the subject is not merely clustered or predicted for the purpose of greater insight – the output of that clustering and classification is presented back to the subject, creating a recursive element to the classification. We are algorithmically encouraged to become more like our classified selves, to progress at a learning rate toward the local minima like a gradient descent algorithm, or, to use the Kafka-inspired term from Chapter 4, to 'embrace the suit'.

Optimization emphasizes 'knowing' and efficiency over the autonomy of messy, chaotic pluralistic unknowability. The desire to reduce the risk and anxiety of 'not knowing' is a human instinct, but it is also a market imperative. For example, the need of many who long for a nostalgic, homogeneous, comprehensible past is not simply an impulse, it is a marketing strategy. Companies use nostalgia to sell products in several ways. These include relaunching historical brands, invoking a brand's heritage to connect it to an imagined past, and branding objects as 'vintage' to capitalize on consumers high valuation of the past (Dam et al 2024). Optimization algorithms, with their guarantees of 'knowing', may seem appealing to those who want to retrieve a fictionalized golden age of certainty. The politics of recovery, of combating an era of moral decay, of spiritual decline, or of the perceived loss of social welfare or public safety or national identity, is going to be aided by a politics of classification. It is also going to more easily identify those consumers who are open to a 'retro marketing' appeal.

The politics of classification is the politics of abstracting identities and encouraging them towards acting more like their abstracted online selves through repeated engagement with recommendation algorithms (learning toward the local minima), hence reinforcing a sense of epistemological certainty. Market imperatives drive a need for subjects to be placed definitively in one category, be it cultural, aesthetic, lifestyle-driven, class-based, ethno-national or racial. It reinforces the idea that your abstract category is a prime determinant of what you are. That an algorithmically ordained category might overlap with historical or empirically generated categories is a secondary concern. In either case, the politics of classification more clearly defines the distinction between in-group and out-group. It reinforces the idea of homogeneity by presuming that if you are in this box, you cannot be in that box.

This varies wildly from the assumptions of the Austrian economists that buyers and sellers are agents on a level playing field looking to buy or sell goods. Sellers in markets can adjust prices such that they meet the subjective needs of enough buyers for sellers to profit and for buyers to gain value. Given adequate competition, sellers are constantly pushed to lower costs or improve the prospective value of their goods. Buyers and sellers can then arrive at the magic 'Pareto optimal' point at which both buyer and seller are optimally satisfied with a transaction. Yet, when algorithms manipulate price signals based on data-driven insights into buyer behaviour, the natural balance of market forces risks becoming distorted, reducing individuals' agency in making authentic choices.

Pareto optimality is a strong argument for the free market. One view is that state spending on goods constitutes a form of coercion because it is impossible to arrive at a consensus on what 'society' needs (Hayek 2007). According to this view, social problems are best left to the free market, where individuals apply their subjective value to construct a life they find meaningful and rewarding, free from the interference of a maximalist state. This is a core principle of classical liberalism. Yet, in an environment where algorithms nudge individual behaviour and shape desires, the distinction between coercion by the state and coercion by algorithms becomes blurred, threatening the very freedom Hayek sought to protect.

There is a fundamental tension between Hayek's view that markets produce Pareto optimal outcomes and the actual uses of algorithms to distort markets (Pasquale 2015). The impact of algorithms on market competition and innovation has been a subject of growing concern among researchers and policy makers. Several studies suggest that algorithms may indeed reinforce monopolies and undermine competition in various ways. Algorithms can maximize prices without directly colluding with competitors (Calvano et al 2020). In 2023, the US Department of Justice (DOJ) brought a suit against RealPage, a company that uses an algorithm called YieldStar on vast amounts of data to suggest daily prices for open units (Vogell 2022). The DOJ contended that the company allowed landlords to share information about rental rates and lease terms to PageRank which it could then use to generate pricing recommendations for other clients, creating tacit coordination that the DOJ alleged constituted collusion. The DOJ alleged that 'automating an anticompetitive scheme does not make it less anticompetitive' (Vogell 2022). A former prosecutor in the DOJ's antitrust division characterized how algorithms collude: '[M]achines quickly learn the only way to win is to push prices above competitive levels' (Stucke in Vogell 2022).

The assumptions of classical economics become strained under the shift toward 'intangible capital' (Haskel and Westlake 2022). Tangible capital comprises physical infrastructure like machinery and buildings, towards intangible capital (research, design, branding and algorithms). Intangible capital has specific attributes referred to as the '4 S's': scalability (the ability of intangible assets to be scaled easily, as with applying algorithms on massive datasets), sunken-ness (the fact that intangible assets often have little value if a firm fails – for example, if a firm fails to collect data, its algorithms are of limited value), synergies (the tendency of the value of intangible assets to increase exponentially in value when bought together or in combination – that is, expanding access to different varieties of data), and spillovers (the benefits that intangible assets can have for outside firms – for example, data brokers selling data to other firms) (Haskel and Westlake 2022, 3). The shift to an intangible capital economy favours the formation of monopolies. Scalability and synergies benefit incumbent firms. Large firms can gain higher returns from intangible investments than small ones. Rather than innovate in-house, firms can buy up innovative promising firms and build up a monopoly-like portfolio of intangible assets.

This has produced a growing call for anti-trust regulation. The nomination of Lina Khan as chair of the Federal Trade Commission during the Biden administration in the United States and the European Union's Digital Markets Act, which seeks to regulate and limit the market-shaping ability of large Internet platforms, are examples of the shifting politics of regulation (Haskel and Westlake 2022). This monopoly formation in the economy has led to 'algorithmically induced mark-ups, low innovation, poor management and employment practices, rent-seeking, and dissatisfied consumers with nowhere else to go' (Haskel and Westlake 2022, 7). One blaring example of how intangible capital can lead to conglomeration is in the use of algorithms for pricing.

The minimalist state, goes the prevailing view of the last half century, unleashes the entrepreneurial spirit in society. This spirit compels individuals to identify and act upon opportunities to create value. Through trial and error, innovation, and adaptation to changing conditions, committed and persistent entrepreneurs will eventually find the opportunity that turns a profit. The profit motive is crucial, as it drives entrepreneurs to pursue value opportunities, creating win–win situations where buyers get a good that they value, and sellers make a profit. However, in an age of algorithmically driven markets, entrepreneurs may find themselves not innovating freely but adapting to patterns that algorithms dictate, reducing the organic, spontaneous competition that Austrian economists cherish.

The rise of this algorithmically manipulated economy is a form of 'technofeudalism', driven by 'cloud capital' that use its intangible assets (algorithms) to influence consumer behaviour, creating a feedback loop where consumers train the algorithm to train them, leading to a recursive spiral of desire and consumption (Varoufakis 2024). Markets have been replaced by digital platforms like Amazon, Google and Facebook that, rather than encourage Pareto optimality or market efficiency, extract rents from producers and consumers.

Classical economists are concerned with state-led efforts to intervene in the market through price controls, taxes, and regulations because they often lead to market distortions that can negatively impact market prices, reduce efficiency and innovation, and lead to outcomes like unemployment among unskilled workers. This is evident, for example, in the view that minimum wage laws inadvertently increase unemployment among those they aim to help (even if the evidence is not as clear). Austrian economists prefer the 'signalling mechanisms' of the free market. Signalling mechanisms play a vital role in coordinating decentralized decision-making. Prices serve as a form of knowledge, transmitting valuable information about scarcity, preferences, and opportunities. When prices change, they convey this information, prompting individuals to adjust their production, consumption, and innovation accordingly. An example is the rise and fall of trends like Silly Bandz, a brief fad where pre-teens and adolescents furiously collected rubber bands of various shapes, where price signals guide market behaviour. Yet, if algorithms manipulate these signals and personalize market trends based on asymmetrical data advantages, the natural flow of information becomes skewed, undermining the decentralized decision-making that Austrian economics relies upon.

Constructing algorithmic desire

Algorithms do not leave consumer choice to fate. Engagement algorithms are deployed to 'manipulate desire' to fit the needs of modern capitalist consumption (Flisfeder 2021). Flisfeder (2021) criticizes the view that social media is to blame for societal collapse, preferring to see social media as a metaphor for neoliberal capitalism. The dictates of neoliberal capitalism produce strong incentives for us to become 'entrepreneurial, neoliberal subjects' who view ourselves as commodities, brands, data points (Flisfeder 2021, 88–112). Viewed from this framework, algorithms are *desire-producing* not simply *desire-responding*.

The platform generates possibilities for us. We cannot only express voice but potentially commodify that voice. This sense of ourselves as 'brands' is only accelerating. A recent survey found that 65 per cent of Gen Z in the United States consider themselves 'content creators' (YouTube 2024). While some want to express voice, 57 per cent in a recent poll say they explicitly want to be 'influencers' as a career. That number only drops to 41 per cent of all respondents. This despite the fact that less than half of social media influencers earn $15,000 a year from being an influencer (Morning Consult 2023).

This cycle of constant influencing and being influenced is anxiety provoking. Flisfeder (2021) argues that social media promises to resolve the *lack* we feel as selves in a capitalist structure – a fundamental absence or desire for something we do not have (Lacan 1988). When these platforms cannot address the lack, individuals react by becoming cynical. They blame the inability to have lack fulfilled (and created) by social media or other institutions (politics, corporations, and so on) The term 'doom spending' has appeared in a number of news articles to describe mindless online shopping that 'self-soothes' pessimistic Gen Z-ers and Millennials who have lost faith in the economic and political systems (Bhaimiya 2024).

When we post into the void, we feel unseen – 'the compulsion to (re)tweet is the symptom of our need to feel affective recognition from the other' (Flisfeder 2021, 86). But this is a treadmill. Influencers describe the burnout they suffer from having to produce so much content. The influenced have only so much money they can spend on products that can satisfy this lack. Hence both influencers and the influenced ultimately become dissatisfied. Engagement on social media does not satisfy the lack in the same way that scratching a bug bite does not make it go away. Indeed, fulfilment of lack would render the algorithm useless since lack is what drives technocapitalist production and consumption. The algorithm both witnesses and shapes our desires (Flisfeder 2021).

Because the algorithm cannot deliver what we need, our efforts to satisfy lack becomes perverse (Flisfeder 2021). There is not an identifiable 'other' to resist against, so we construct an imaginary other that we can 'transgress' against. We create enemies online that give us the pleasure and satisfaction of thinking we are 'transgressing authority' when it is in reality more grist for the neoliberal data collection and analysis system mill (Flisfeder 2021). Transgressing against an unspecified other is ultimately unsatisfying – 'we can never fully determine what the other desires leaving us dependent upon a metonymy of desire, without solution' (Black 2023, 2). This frustration makes us cynical, and we turn to distorted and perverse ways to satisfy desire – we troll, we shame, we 'cancel' as an effort to give meaning to our online lives. But it is all performative rebellion which is then repackaged as data for capital accumulation.

This is the dark side of the algorithmic contract. The promise of the contract is to give us a 'new identity' online that will help us find meaning.

When that 'new identity' is unable to satisfy our desires, we do not log off. Our ability to find meaning in the larger society has also been diminished. Instead, our desire seeking and meaning making becomes distorted into serving the needs of a psychotic libidinal economy (Lacan 1988) where the normal lines between fantasy and reality are blurred or broken down. We have an awareness of the futility of 'screaming into our keyboards'. Yet there is some distorted attraction to the abstracted, synthetic reality of the algorithmic contract. It is a perverse, libidinal state that we embrace through negative affect – using and sharing demeaning, insulting, trolling, and abusive content.

The era of surveillance advertising

The 'inherently perverse' cynicism of users Flisfeder (2021, 186) describes extends beyond social media. We are a decade into the era of 'platform capitalism' (Srnicek 2017). A platform represents a 'digital infrastructures that enable interactions between two or more groups' (Srnicek 2017, 43). Rather than building a marketplace from the ground up, a platform provides the necessary infrastructure to intervene in existing markets and upend market relations. Examples of such platforms include Google for searching, Uber for taxis, and Facebook for social networking. What makes platform capitalism distinct is that Uber owns few cars and has no drivers on its payroll and yet is one of the largest 'taxi' companies in the world. This is what makes it attractive – its 'leanness' means that users with a car can be plugged in to the platform and make money as a 'side hustle' while providing riders with an affordable transit option. The answer to Uber's success lies in its core function, which revolves around extracting and using a particular kind of raw material – user data. Users are the natural source of this raw material, much like oil in the industrial age, but they are also consumers.

The futility and cynicism that Flisfeder (2021) finds on social media has parallels in the gig economy. Platforms like Uber and Airbnb promote deregulation and gig economy models, which can lead to labour exploitation and reduced job security (Srnicek 2017). These platforms embody a neoliberal economic model that prioritizes flexibility and efficiency over traditional labour protections. The effect is to produce overworked, underpaid gig workers who, in turn, largely grow more cynical about an economy that does not address their *lack* monetarily and a politics that seems feckless in its ability to address the inequities present in the platform economy.

Meanwhile, the value of platforms increases with the number of users they acquire. This creates a positive feedback loop that can lead to monopolistic tendencies (Srnicek 2017). Platforms can develop data advantages that allow them to optimize profit (for example, Uber and Lyft can better model surge pricing because of their massive databases of riders than upstarts could).

Additionally, platforms often practice cross-subsidization, where one arm of the firm reduces the price of a service or goods, even providing them for free, while another arm raises prices to compensate for these losses. For example, Amazon Web Services and Google AdSense help offset losses from new ventures that struggle initially to make a profit.

There is a gold rush to become the next 'platform star'. Each year, the Consumer Electronics Show in Las Vegas rolls out a new generation of 'Internet of Things' devices. In 2017, these devices included a smart saltshaker, a smart hairbrush and a smart toaster. The existence of and market for these 'smart' things reflects the current 'data gold rush' era. Each of these devices produces data points and combined with other data, promise to make you more predictable. The fact that, as humans, we have an endless capacity to produce data, makes us a resource for a commodity, much like a reservoir is a resource for extracting oil (Toonders 2014). But unlike the reservoir, we have thoughts and feelings about our commodified data.

Data collection devices are not limited to hairbrushes and toasters. The emerging 'smart cities' movement promotes a philosophy of 'smartness' (or optimization) in urban space (Halpern and Mitchell 2023). Cities are replete with 'smartness' both physically (fibre optic cables, satellite data, server farms) and ubiquitously through monitoring devices. Using public space for enhancing 'smartness' (optimization of goals like security or efficiency) by installing cameras and other monitoring devices changes how we interact in physical space. Data collection becomes ubiquitous and our desire to 'fit the model' and 'move to the local minima' extends beyond the social media platform to how we interact in public space.

This move towards 'smart cities' extends the algorithmic contract beyond social media. It promises the optimized city that can be enjoyed without fear of crime or discomfort. This algorithmic management feeds into the belief that the world out there can be controlled, which in turn fuels a desire for even more control. This desire for control is further stoked by a ubiquitous surveillance industry. This formulation of 'smartness' as the philosophy of our 'datafied' culture accelerates concerns of an overarching 'philosophy of the algorithm' that undermines individual and group autonomy but is quite lucrative to those engaged in selling algorithmic security.

Smart cities also produce an 'advertising technology ecosystem' (Tau 2024). In this ecosystem, ad exchanges and brokers compete for advertising space, but they also scoop up data from various apps. While cell phones have matured as data sources, the focus is now shifting toward cars and Bluetooth data. This presents a moving target, as people become more aware of these practices. Companies like Apple have responded to events like the Cambridge Analytica scandal by shutting down APIs (application programming interfaces) and limiting data access. However, the use of data capturing devices is only increasing. Many of these devices are sold to citizens as *smartness* tools that will optimize the experience of the city.

This also produces a paradoxical effect. When things in the optimized city do not go as planned, the frustration only inspires more algorithmic solutionism. The lack of getting the precise thing a customer wants may lead to rude interactions, which is then recorded and posted on social media for everyone to comment upon. Each transgression, like a smash and grab robbery, is recorded and posted on social media, which then motivates some to engage in more extravagant and outrageous public behaviour that can be recorded on a smartphone, posted on social media, and commodified if an influencer reposts it. This incentivizes social media users to treat others as material for algorithmic recognition and social media enjoyment rather than as dignity-deserving humans.

This depersonalization of 'the other' is central to surveillance capitalism – the 'deeply intentional and highly consequential new logic of accumulation' (Zuboff 2019, 1). The world of ubiquitous data collection produces endless opportunities for removing humans from the transaction. This can range from the difficulty inherent in getting to speak to a human on a customer service call to more pernicious ones. Zuboff (2019, 81) envisions a future where automated devices, controlled remotely, allow for the disabling of a rented car if payments are missed, driving it back to the leaser without ever notifying the customer. The shift towards automated enforcement of contracts reduces risk by 'emptying contracts of uncertainty' (Zuboff 2019, 81). In this example, disabling a car for missing payments and eventually driving it back to the leaser reduces the messiness of the customer's pleas for an extension or the legitimate excuses they may have for not making payments. There is a science fiction impersonality to such transactions that makes life nastier for customers but makes transactions more optimal for companies.

Surveillance capitalism is sold as the optimization of everyday life, but what sustains it is 'surveillance advertising' – collecting, analysing and selling users' data for the purpose of advertising (Crain 2021). This shift to the user as commodity was not inevitable. Zuckerman (2014) calls this shift from a 'neutral' Internet to one built upon surveillance advertising the 'original sin' of the Internet. The incentive structure of surveillance advertising is to become more persistent and more invasive in the effort to compete against rivals for more useful data. The better this data is for prediction and influence, the more valuable it becomes. While data has always been an important element of advertising, this 'race for data' spurred on by the ubiquity of the digital, is akin to the gold rush in the United States in the mid-19th century (Crain 2021) – a frontier that was eventually tamed – where a handful of companies become consolidated under monopolistic or oligopolistic control (Wu 2011).

The roots of the modern algorithmic contract start with the various efforts to monetize Internet users. Early advertising efforts like the 'pop-up' ad (Zuckerman 2014) and the 'banner ad' (Crain 2021) were not effective, partly because they were transparent as advertising and annoying to users. Users in turn could use ad blocking software to avoid seeing them. As technology evolved, so did the techniques to reach consumers. Interstitial and rich media ads became more effective ways to force users to view ad content (Crain 2021). But the advent of the 'cookie' introduced the idea of surreptitious consumer tracking. Tech companies could track users, collect data on their habits, and serve them more targeted ads in a way that was not intrusive to the user. What companies did with the user's data was not of immediate concern to someone who just wanted to watch a video or visit a website. In exchange for the seemingly 'ad free' experience, users traded access to their habits (their data).

This surreptitious advertising model was accelerated by the emergence of pay-per-click advertising (Crain 2021). Google soon adopted a tool called AdWords where advertisers could bid on keywords for the privilege of having their ads appear when users search for those terms. That innovation encouraged using algorithms and machine learning to 'narrow-target' consumers. Surveillance advertising led to the profit taking that made today's tech monopolies.

The pay-per-click model changed the incentive structure of the Internet, incentivizing salacious or incendiary content that would attract attention and hence receive more 'clicks'. The incentive for platforms was to create apps and websites that encourages frequent engagement through the building of online communities of interest. Rather than rely on experts, Internet platforms began to rely on the 'the wisdom of the crowd', a phenomenon Jaron Lanier (2006) called 'digital Maoism' – that is, the collectivization of labour without compensating the creators. For example, food critics would be supplanted by an army of Yelp reviews, editorial pages by Reddit discussions, and music critics by Spotify algorithms. Focusing on the 'crowd' over the expert made it cheaper for platforms to acquire content, which they could then use to attract and engage users. But it also set up the expectation of 'free information' through the replacement of expertise by the crowd. The crowd, through its collective wisdom, could do the same thing the critic once did without anyone having to be paid for the curated expertise. Once the algorithm became more widely used, it created the possibility that the user could 'self-curate' the external world without having to rely on the expert, whose aesthetic discernment took years to cultivate. More importantly, this expert knowledge came with a price – one might have to buy a newspaper or magazine to access it. But with the pay-per-click model, the crowd could provide you with similar expertise for free.

This move towards getting user attention eventually turned towards 'clickbait' and low-quality information flooding platforms and websites. Crain (2021) calls this messaging used to collect more data and sell more products 'manipulative communication'. It has had profound spillover effects on newspapers, who now had to adopt the principles of manipulative communication to capture the advertising dollars that were exclusive to newsprint. Once reputable news organizations have become 'clickbait' companies, creating content for the sole purpose of producing salacious headlines and getting people to engage with the advertising on the page. Any semblance of civic responsibility on the part of news media is consumed whole by the need to compete for eyeballs in a fierce attention economy. This extends to individuals, who, if they want to 'build a brand' on social media, must adhere to the dictates of the algorithm and engage in their own manipulative communication.

This was not fait accompli in the US context, but the result of a lack of regulation and a neoliberal economic climate that saw 'government as the enemy'. Manipulative communication has been with us for most of American history, taking a more pernicious form in the early 20th century with the move towards mass marketing (Crain 2021). Public relations pioneer Edward Bernays had the insight that rather than sell the features of the product, you can attach products to deeper inner drives as a form of manipulative communication (for example, Nike's 'Just do it' ads). The shift from descriptive to affective communication allowed companies to differentiate products that were basically the same by claiming different metaphors and aspirations.

Technoliberalism and the cybercultural frontier

This optimization logic and the algorithmic contract that supports it are only possible because of our trust in technology. Although it has come under deserved scrutiny in recent years, we still largely subscribe to 'technoliberalism', defined by Fish as 'a left-liberal, deterministic, utopian digital discourse ... [which] claims that a faith in networked technology can ameliorate the contradictions of an ideology that includes both economic and social liberalism' (Fish in Jenkins 2017).

Technology is not merely a tool; it is central to the development of modern capitalism. It emphasizes coordination among tech elites and their capitalist funders rather than competition. It promises to use neoliberal solutions to address progressive liberal problems (Fish 2017). It does so in practice by absorbing previously non-market relationships into economic activity. One core example might be the use of dating apps to commodify the intimacy of personal relationships. Under technoliberalism, everything becomes subsumed under the optimization task. I wrote back in 2012 about how

Facebook took the private, non-market activity of maintaining connections with family and close friends and made them public with the aim of making them commercial relations (how that commodification would pan out was still an open question a decade ago) (Marichal 2012).

This insight is not entirely new. Marcuse (1964) saw mid-20th century Western culture as the 'commodification of reality' where more and more aspects of everyday life get enveloped in this process of desire and status fulfilment. This is not a coerced system, but one in which individuals willingly submit. Throughout the 20th century, we have seen an increased 'democratization of desire' where individuals are encouraged by advertising to covet luxury goods and the social status that comes from their conspicuous consumption (Veblen 1899). This shift from pre-enlightenment societies where roles were fixed to one where the individual self-governs makes individuals more susceptible to desire manipulation. We subscribe to an 'economic gospel of consumption' where the expectation is that consumption will produce happiness and social status (Cowdrick 1927).

What is different is the application of algorithms to this impulse. Marcuse was optimistic that citizens would see through the banality of a 'commodified reality'. This is what drove the 1960s counterculture (in part). But it is harder to resist algorithmic commodification since it is difficult to see, unlike the magazine ad or billboard. Once commodified, a previously 'slow' analogue relationship falls into the optimization mandate and becomes 'efficient' and optimized. But optimized towards what? Which friend's posts should you see? Which news content will keep you engaged? I had lunch some time ago with an old friend I had not seen in over a decade. In her typical bluntness, she asked me at lunch why I never responded to her Facebook posts. I was flummoxed since I was not even sure we were Facebook friends. I would not deliberately avoid her, but she perceived me as snubbing her. When I returned to my hotel, I looked through my Facebook feed and, sure enough, there were no posts from her. But when I looked her up, I found dozens of posts that simply never came across my feed.

Why did I not see her posts? I will likely never know. She is someone who posts about 'small things': a cup of tea she made or a work of crochet she had just finished. These are things that I do not normally like or comment upon. Because of this, I had seemingly been classified as someone who would not be interested in posts about crochet and tea. The hegemonic logic that technical systems can be managed and optimized by algorithm had decided which friends were important for me to keep tabs on and which were not. But at no point did I make the independent choice that I wanted to exclude viewing my friend's posts. The default in this case is to automate my relationships to this friend in ways the algorithm perceives as 'optimal'. I do not comment on or like posts about crochet, so the algorithm surmises I do not want to know what my friend is up to. It will present me with posts about friends with which I share more hobbies in common. But 'optimizing' friendships would not be my choice.

It is through engagement with one another that things adopt their meaning. Otherwise, everything is a signifier. Everything is a subjective identity marker. If artifacts have a politics embedded in them, then the engagement algorithm optimizes for turning everything into a consumer choice, including one's empirical engagement with the world. We are being 'engineered' as if we were architecture. This is easy to see with the built environment. An architect is going to have designs about how the people in a building should behave. Different spaces are designed to create different moods and habits in people. The great cathedrals of Europe are designed to inspire awe and reverence. But the algorithm's status as an artifact is more concealed. If a tool of technology is engaged in 'architecting the mind', it is hard to see the engineering at work the way you might be able to see with a building. There is no visible scaffolding. Inside a building, you can reflect on the space, and you can reflect on the effect the space is having on you. There is no such guidance with algorithmic engineering.

AI promises to turbo-charge this process of 'mind engineering'. While some express concern about the pace of AI development, techno-optimists tout the promise of AI's capacity, which include the discovery of new, cheaper energy sources and exponential growth in productivity through AI-discovered design and manufacturing processes (Suleyman 2023). Shariatmadari (2023) summarizes the AI utopian vision of one founder, along with its perils:

> If the printing press allowed ordinary people to own books, and the silicon chip put a computer in every home, AI will democratize simply doing things. So, sure, that means getting a virtual assistant to set up a company for you or using a swarm of builder bots to throw up an extension. Unfortunately, it also means engineering a run on a bank or creating a deadly virus using a DNA synthesizer.

This is a new iteration of technoliberalism. Private sector ingenuity will address progressive liberal problems much better than the state ever would. The United Nations' 'AI for Good' initiative attempts to tie AI discovery to the 17 United Nations development goals. This tension between the state and technoliberalism pits empowerment through political mobilization and engagement with formal institutions of the state against the view that 'the consumer has more power for good or ill than the voter' (Morozov 2014). This latter perspective emphasizes empowerment through the production and use of technological tools, reflecting a belief in the transformative potential of technology. According to this view, when technology, such as computers, becomes accessible to everyone, it enables a form of democratization and revolution. The algorithmic contract is rooted in technoliberal assumptions about the prospects of technology to solve social problems. Technoliberalism promises to provide users with autonomy through skill development and the social connection that comes from collaboration on social problems (Illich in Morozov 2014). It promises a world where 'the philosopher goes to work and the working man becomes a philosopher', promoting a society where individuals gain personal meaning through making and learning new skills (Illich in Morozov 2014).

Tools of suspicion

Instead of personal growth tools, algorithms have given us *tools of suspicion*. The politics of optimization and classification make for vigilant consumers promised the ability to reduce risk from harm by imagined threats through increased access to 'smart technologies' that monitor our environment. Our modern era is characterized by a sense of danger and paranoia – what Woo (2002) called 'stochastic terrorism'. The sense of uncertainty is engineered through the algorithmic contract. Optimization prioritizes decisions that eliminate contingency. What causes someone to feel secure is the ability to feel as if they understand the world around them. The algorithmic contract both presents the conditions for stochastic terror and provides users with the tools they can use to reduce their anxiety about this synthetically augmented 'terror-filled' world. As adults, we know that the real world is not reassuring – it is full of doubt and contingency. Algorithmic classification through things like engagement/recommendation algorithms can have the effect of narrowing one's ontological/epistemological perspective into pre-set categories that reduce anxiety and provide comfort that the 'prismatic' world presented to users through the algorithm is the same as the world 'out there'. In this algorithmic classification society, the outlier who does not want to have a prismatic perspective on the world fights an uphill battle to receive a meaningful, balanced information diet. The outlier becomes a source of anxiety and threat.

Stochastic terror can also be an effective tool for data collection. Tools designed to address this perceived terror are a form of 'luxury surveillance' (Gilliard 2022). Devices like Ring cameras, placed outside a home's front door, allow continuous monitoring of the immediate environment. This constant access reinforces a world of ambient stochastic terror by keeping people on guard to any change in pattern that might occur in their neighbourhood, such as a 'suspicious character' on the street whose presence needs to be removed. In many ways, these devices turn us into 'citizen anomaly detectors' who engage in our own, less efficient, optimization exercises. In a real sense, we become 'optimization machines' searching for 'outliers' that would presumably threaten us.

Luxury surveillance products fuel the drive we have to 'know the unknowable'. Algorithms encourage the fostering of a classification mindset that cues us into 'ambient threat' and promises safety if we employ these devices. This surveillance-driven *classification economy* further entrenches the problem of the outlier. There are new dangers, particularly for marginalized groups, for 'acting anomalously' by walking through a residential neighbourhood with an armada of Ring cameras and a NextDoor account. With a culture of ambient surveillance fuelled by the threat of stochastic terror, those who want to deviate from the norm become increasingly visible and potentially stigmatized, lessening their desire to do novel things and impacting their autonomy and independent decision-making.

The combination of Ring Cameras and NextDoor in many ways is frustrating (and sub-optimal) to law enforcement because it potentially criminalizes a much broader range of activity that distracts police resources from serious and genuine criminal activity. In my own conversation with a local city manager, he brought up the ways in which the local social media app NextDoor drives a lot of the city government's agenda. The city is forced to spend ample amounts of time having to deal with perceived stochastic terror complaints from residents in ways that distract them from addressing real problems in the community. This algorithmic-driven classification society creates a self-reinforcing cycle where arbitrarily clustered subjects spend time being 'anomaly detectors'. Those who do not conform to perceived norms become hyper-scrutinized in ways that encourage many to conform or take it upon themselves to reduce the signal-to-noise ratio.

Stochastic terror is not reserved solely for our Ring cameras. Increasingly, we see the world through the lens of order and disorder and engage in this type of mentality on a more personal basis. Data collection tools give you the promise of having your worldview confirmed or having your anxieties allayed. Paradoxically, this customization of your digital life creates even more anxiety because when actual stochastic world events that are inconsistent with your worldview occur, they become even more puzzling. This treadmill of identifying threats and addressing them becomes a 'whack-a-mole' exercise in exhaustion – an exhaustion that can also be addressed through the purchase of more luxury surveillance tools.

We do not just monitor external threats; we also monitor ourselves. One example might be the use of Fitbits or Apple watches for monitoring steps or monitoring heart rate – events that are associated with the 'self-quantification' movement that has existed for over a decade (Lupton 2016). Once upon a time, someone with high blood pressure might go to their doctor, find out their blood pressure is a bit high, and modify their diet. Now, the same person can monitor their blood pressure with a fitness watch on a 24/7 basis.

Usually, watches come with a monthly paid service that will track or provide more information or help you optimize towards a goal. We are optimizing towards a goal that no one is directly forcing us to adopt but we do so nonetheless because we are driven to relieve anxiety. This self-optimization comes directly from the classification economy's insistence on ranking and comparing us to one another.

Gilliard (2022) makes the interesting observation that Fitbits collect much more data on its users than do ankle monitors. On its face, this may seem illogical, since the ankle monitor is supposed to be collecting data on people who have been accused of or have committed a crime. But it speaks of the ways in which we have bought in to the algorithmic contract. We have traded the promise of optimization to an algorithmically set standard in exchange for becoming the subject of data surveillance. This willingness to be surveilled and sorted by the data we produce feeds back into the classification economy, further grouping and classifying us based on our data.

Amazon's hardware chief Dave Limp refers to 'ambient intelligence' – the presence of technologies that operate in the background but are always present, collecting information and processing that information. He describes these technologies as ones that will empower customers to engage in other tasks: 'Today, ambient intelligence comes to life across all of our devices and services, working behind the scenes on customers' behalf, so they can focus on the here and now, and the people and experiences that matter most to them' (Wilhelm and Kellner 2022). The classification economy has the effects of normalizing a surveillance society where, because we perceive the benefits of reducing stochastic terror, we allow ourselves to be monitored 24/7. The optimization task is often seen as an impersonal exercise. One obvious reason for this is that data does not have a soul. It does not tell a story. A story must be imposed upon it from outside. Optimization is a story of certitude. The resistance to optimization is to turn to narrative, humanizing allegory, to turn a metaphorical life into a literal one: 'To think abstract problems through on several planes at the same time, to stay alert for symbolic and allegorical meanings, to appreciate the utility of nuance – as opposed to living a literal life, where most things mean in only one way' (Lopez 2020).

A metaphorical life is nuanced, sub-optimal and bad for business. Narrative and metaphor can have the effect of challenging classification by presenting alternative accounts of what the anomalous case means. A literal life is a Manichean existence, dividing the world into those who share our classification and those who are classified as 'other'. In this optimized world, 'things only mean in one way'. We can intellectually understand how a *literal life* of optimization leads to the erasure of the subjectivity of human experience. The application of the optimization/classification problem uncritically and unfeelingly towards fellow humans or towards other living things runs the risk of mis-recognizing subjects as something other than who they are (Taylor 1994). But more perniciously, it runs the risk of truncating our imaginations regarding who we can become, all for the sake of being more predictable, stochastically terrified, consumers.

Algorithms, in their efforts to classify us, operate primarily within a synthetic reality. We can choose to disconnect: to put down the phone and unplug from the virtual world. Yet, we cannot fully unplug. We feel our data viscerally (Lupton 2016). We produce data as we go through our daily lives, and we engage with the classified outputs of our data through our senses. The clicks and beeps of our devices elicit a real-world response from us. The chime of social media notifications creates a limbic system response (Lupton 2016). To claim that we could separate ourselves from the virtual world is to suggest an individualized solution to a collective problem. The real issue lies in how we are incentivized, through consumer culture, to act in ways that reinforce our classifications. How does the vast industry of data brokers perpetuate this? This synthetic reality created by algorithms contributes to a classification society where our actions are constantly monitored and classified. This exacerbates the problem for those who attempt to disconnect or resist classification, potentially impacting their autonomy and decision-making abilities in both online and offline contexts.

Even if our reality is *prismatic stochastic terror*, the algorithmic contract sells us on the possibility of our own personal utopia. A future society of endless joy and wonder where many of humanity's resource problems have been solved, like Iain Banks' *Culture* series of novels (Orbit Books, 1987–2012). It is no accident that Elon Musk is a fan of these books (Power 2022). A 'society of joy' in a science-fiction future might also be one where we are perfectly classified and ordered, a futuristic 'republic of virtue' where the challenge becomes identifying those who might disrupt or question this fun, those who might act in unpredictable ways.

One example I like to use in classes comes from the political philosopher Robert Nozick's (1974, 42) 'experience machine' (or 'pleasure machine'). He posits a thought experiment that speculated upon whether, if we could strap ourselves into a machine that would gratify all our desires, we would we choose that over the disappointments and contingencies of life. Would we accept techno-authoritarianism if it came to us in the form of a pleasure machine, allowing us to pursue our private pleasures with the caveat that we would not challenge the state when we disagree with it? This thought experiment highlights the potential consequences of an algorithmic classification society, where the problem of the outlier becomes acute for those who choose not to participate in the pleasure machine, potentially facing severe limitations on their autonomy and ability to make independent decisions outside of the prescribed system. More relevant to our modern lives is how we treat others that do not bring us pleasure or comfort. How do we react when we inevitably leave the pleasure machine and enter the messy contingent world as it is. Remaining an algorithmic problem is a rejection of pleasure machines that seek to optimize us towards an abstract, synthetic ontological reality.

6

Optimizing Identity

In the preface of his famous *Leaves of Grass*, Walt Whitman produces a manifesto in defence of individual autonomy. The poem represents an insistence on being present to the wonders of the world, to approach others with openness and humility, and to question orthodoxy. He instructs readers to 'dismiss whatever insults your own soul, and your very flesh shall be a great poem' (Whitman 1855). This mythologizing of individualism is central to the American ethos. It is also part of what makes the algorithmic contract valid in the eyes of American people.

In many ways, the culture of Silicon Valley is consistent with the view of the American Romantics. Ralph Waldo Emerson, the son of Puritan clergy, broke from the collaborative, civic minded view of the Massachusetts Puritans. He was a champion of individualism over communitarianism. Individuals, for Emerson, must take care to not succumb to the conformity of groupthink, but rather to 'insist on yourself'. (Emerson 1841, 51). This view differed from the traditional views of Puritan pastors like Ezra Ripley, who objected to this core principle of 'self-reliance': 'Who could live alone and independent? Who but some disgusted hermit or half-crazy enthusiast will say to society, I have no need of thee; I am under no obligation to my fellow-men?' (Fuhrer 2014, 28).

The American transcendentalist idea constitutes a radical departure from viewing the self primarily as part of a social order. Emerson's denunciation of community norms can seem anarchist at times, as when he declares in 'Self-Reliance', 'society everywhere is in conspiracy against the manhood of its members'(Emerson 1841, 14). This prioritization of the sacredness of the individual and their unique experience is central to the algorithmic contract. The appeal of finding and understanding our own minds, our own authentic selves, is what the algorithmic world promises. But the algorithmic contract, while it sells us a transcendental individualist freedom, ultimately undermines this search for an authentic self.

The belief that the transcendent exists in nature and in the divine spark of human beings through a deep moral sense is a double-edged sword. It is impossible to divorce oneself from one's social environment. The key point of the transcendentalists was to argue that humans are in touch with the divine when they humble themselves before the awe and wonder of nature (including the self) and properly recognize the limitations of human institutions. This view does not call for ignoring authority but encourages healthy scepticism above unquestioning obedience. Rather than transcendentalism serving as a license for narcissism, it is a recognition of the inability of humans to fully comprehend the world they live in. Failure to recognize the complexity and fullness of the world is failure to tap into the 'divine spark'.

Individualism has always been a contested idea in American thought. Emerson's perspective stood in contrast to Alexis de Tocqueville's (2006) concerns about the *levelling* impulses of democracy. While Emerson critiqued the notion that Americans were truly politically equal, suggesting there was 'too little democracy' in the emerging United States, Tocqueville was concerned that the extension of democratic rights could create resentment when the perception of economic and social equality inevitably does not produce equality for all. Indeed, we can trace citizens' lack of trust in institutions to the unrealized promise that came with the democratization of voice through social media. That resentment is the opposite of the divine spark. It is a wilful extinguishing of that which is transcendent within us as subjects. The algorithmic contract, however, is a promise of actualization that often leads to resentment and cynicism.

Techno-romanticism

Our age would seem custom made for transcendentalism. Facebook co-founder Mark Zuckerberg's ethos of 'move fast and break things' would seem to bear a facile similarity to Emerson's romantic notions of self-listening to the 'divine spark' (although Emerson was famously sceptical of technological progress). Emerson was preoccupied with the burgeoning United States creating its own ethos, noting in an address to Harvard's Phi Beta Kappa society that Americans have 'listened too long to the courtly muses of Europe' (Emerson 1837), insisting that they must cultivate an American ethos rooted in individualism rather than conformity and obedience.

Silicon Valley culture is often described as libertarian, but I think that philosophy lacks the spirit of romanticism present in techno-optimism. People like Ray Kurzweil (2005) and his concept of the singularity represent a mythic attachment to science and technology as vehicles for human emancipation. Even the current debates about 'rogue AI' destroying civilization has a mytho-poetic resonance. Emerson advocated for not being a servant to convention but instead following the 'inner compass' or 'divine spark' within each person, where nature and God were intertwined.

Unlike American pragmatists, American romantics see truth as not coming from community or scientific consensus, but through individual human experience and divine intuition. Indeed, the needs of the community can often get in the way of the cultivation of an 'inner spark'.

Techno-romanticism would embrace this elevation of the individual, the maverick pathbreaker who promises a 'new life' in modernity that introduces the possibility that just around the corner something will free you from the misfortunes of this fraught existence (Beer 2022). This 'myth of a new life' always *in the future* can be applied to all technological advances, from nuclear fusion to nanotechnology to AI. Embedded in their appeal is the belief that the next discovery will significantly alleviate human suffering and open up a world of possibility. This is all only possible via technoliberalism.

This techno-romanticism is part of the culture of Silicon Valley. Turner (2013) details the shift in Silicon Valley from counterculture to cyberculture. The cyberculture view is that social problems are best handled by entrepreneurs with a professional engineering mindset where the goal is task optimization. This was a romanticized notion with young, tech-savvy teens in the 1980s buying Stewart Brand's *Whole Earth Catalog* and tinkering with engineering kits and early computers. Through engineering and computer programming, you could 'geek' your way to your own utopia. The premise was that if you just free people up to build things and just let the market take care of your needs, you will satisfy your preferences.

The ethos of engineering for cyber culturalists is experienced as *apolitical* – either the bridge collapses or it does not. Coding or software engineering problems are complex enough without having to determine whether there is ethical relevance to 'solving the puzzle'. It is preferable to say 'we're just building the bridge' without having to get into thorny questions of who is responsible for who drives over it safely or who has access to it. Similarly, the algorithmic designer is tasked with 'reducing the cost function', as if mathematical problems do not have a politics, but a romantic transcendence removed from the mundane questions of politics. The engineering mindset can hide any political imperatives or profit-making imperatives that tech platforms might have. The romanticization of the engineering mindset gives Facebook, Google, and other tech companies the appearance of engineering neutrality.

Techno-romanticism is not the romanticism of Thoreau, who harboured a deep scepticism of progress. He famously disdained the invention of the telegraph, questioning what we would truly say to each other if we could talk from one continent or ocean away. His scepticism was not anti-entrepreneurship or anti-discovery. Rather, he doubted whether this knowledge would make human experience significantly better. If Thoreau were alive today, he would likely be horrified at our ubiquitously datafied society, particularly at how the algorithmic contract robs users of their individuality. If being a transcendentalist requires the time and space for reflection to connect you to your divine 'inner spark', few can avail themselves of that space. This is because the true individualist is a problematic outlier that 'goes against the grain', a distinct challenge for the machine learning algorithms trying to classify us. Algorithmic logic prioritizes mitigating risk over human flourishing. Machine learning algorithms are designed to search for 'anomalous behaviour', to find those 'seekers' who are trying to follow their 'inner compass'.

The algorithmic logic of anomaly detection is one in which prediction replaces understanding. There is a distinct difference between classifying for understanding and classifying for prediction. The former acknowledges that classification helps abstract the world in ways that enhance our understanding, which is what social scientists aim to do. The latter focuses on organizing data for profit, often optimizing it for efficiency at the cost of nuance. But understanding connotes a sense of a distinction between the 'known' and the 'unknown'. It sets up a dichotomy where the purpose of the empirical intervention is to 'know' what we do not know. Anomaly detection is an exercise in 'acting without knowing' or even without desiring to know. It is an exercise in automating the process of decision-making in a way that does not necessitate an explanation for why the anomaly exists.

The reality is that there are severe limits to an 'algorithmic order'. The complexity of deep learning algorithms and the 'answers' they produce is impossible to explain. As such, we replace the *will to know* with the *will to automate*. The philosopher George Bataille distinguishes between 'non-knowledge', which we will never be able to discern, and 'the unknown', which at some point may become known to us (Bataille 2001). The idea of the unknown becoming knowable is central to the scientific revolution – we can uncover the nature of the world around us through empirical analysis. Complex convoluted neural networks shift our emphasis from the 'potentially knowable' to 'non-knowledge', something that is beyond our cognitive capacity. An emphasis on the unknowable means that we are not interested in the outlier. We are only interested in the ways in which the outlier in the training data frustrates our ability to optimize, to predict, or to surveil effectively. The incentive in the world of unknowability is to 'solve' the problem of the outlier such that when it is used to detect anomalies, it can be subdued or eliminated without the need for understanding. Rather than seeing individuals for their distinctiveness, their God-created 'divine spark', the algorithmic contract de-emphasizes understanding and the need to know about the other's life experience or world view.

This reduces the power of the vast unknowability of the world – a power that grounds us in our own limitations and mortality. Taleb (2010) describes Umberto Eco's 'anti-library', which represents all the books in one's library that are never read. He muses that there is intrinsic value in the knowledge, insights, and narratives contained in the books themselves regardless of whether they are ever opened. The anti-library represents un-accessed knowledge and understanding. It is a constant reminder of our 'sub-optimality' – a link to our mortality and the inability to know everything about the world. Taleb (2010, 1) says as much when he wryly comments that 'you will accumulate more knowledge and more books as you grow older, and the growing number of unread books on the shelves will look at you menacingly'. Dickinson (2022) reflects upon this mortality describing his own anti-library: '[T]he titles lining my own home remind me that I know little to nothing about cryptography, the evolution of feathers, Italian folklore, illicit drug use in the Third Reich, and whatever entomophagy is'. Algorithmic optimization hides this reality from us. Contained within my devices is an anti-library, but it does not look back at me menacingly. There is no reminder of my finitude, of the unread books that will never leave me alone. What I do not know, I can look up effortlessly. I do not need to be aware of the possibilities that exist in the anti-library; they are not interesting to me. This is the nature of the algorithmic contract – to promote the possibility of 'a new life' in exchange for relieving the anxiety that comes with knowing there is an anti-library of knowledge that I will never read, or selves I will never become.

The ability to control the imaginary of subjects is a key element of algorithmic power. Whomever 'controls the subjunctive' or the production of imagination, gets to imagine what can be done with technology (Hong 2020, 176). Those in positions of authority may cede responsibility for making decisions to algorithms, but not the power to determine what is decided. This distinction between power and decision is critical to understanding how the algorithm is a *socio-technical system* (Trist 1981). If you are a manager and you imagine that workers are stealing from you (and hence undermining your power), you are likely to use the algorithmic apparatus at your disposal to surveil your workers (Hong 2020). Or, if you imagine that the countries are overrun with dangerous 'illegal immigrants', you are more disposed to use the available algorithmic apparatus to create a border surveillance state.

Engagement algorithms control the subjunctive by steering the user towards predictability. Take the example of a young person exploring libertarianism on YouTube. If an optimization algorithm notices a pattern, such as the person engaging with content from the Cato Institute or American Enterprise Institute, it might suggest more related content. Eventually, the algorithm could steer this person towards more niche or extreme ideologies to keep them engaged, such as 'paleo-conservatism' or 'identitarian' influencers. The person, who might have explored libertarianism, debated it with friends, and adopted those elements of it that conformed with experience, now exists in an environment where radical ideas are amplified, shaped primarily by the algorithm's classifications toward more extreme, engageable views.

The consequence is that algorithms, rather than facilitating growth and understanding, push people towards predetermined ideologies based on engagement metrics with the implicit idea that a 'clustered self' is a more reliable consumer product to sell to advertisers or mobilize for protest than a thinking, contingent self – an unclassified *algorithmic problem*.

The reflecting person is a sub-optimal person. Reflection constitutes 'time off the grid' – time that could potentially move the subject further from the local minima. Reflection places us squarely in the enlightenment pose of self-improvement. When children misbehave, parents will chide them by saying 'go to your room and think about your actions'. The idea is that reflection with an 'inner compass' will ultimately lead to improved behaviour (if good behaviour has been properly modelled). A transcendental nature walk without any data-recording devices is a sub-optimal walk from the perspective of data brokers. Thankfully, we do not yet have 'smart nature' the way we have 'smart cities'.

If an algorithm changes your behaviour, it is not readily apparent to you. You cannot reflect on it because you cannot see the algorithm's effect on you. There is no feedback mechanism. Why do we give so much power to the Silicon Valley engineer? Why do we mythologize Silicon Valley? The culture of the engineer taps into the culture of the United States as one of rugged individualism and an appetite for exploration and discovery (Turner 2013). American mythmaking is full of allusion to groups travailing to the Atlantic in search of both riches and purification. The idea that the Puritans came from England to fulfil one of the founders of the Massachusetts Bay Colony, John Winthrop's (1630) 'city upon a hill' vision and be closer to God is a form of utopian project that gets constantly invoked throughout modern American history. The zeal of the Puritans is related to the evangelical zeal of Silicon Valley tech entrepreneurs (Turner 2013).

The frontier is us

The myth of the American Manifest Destiny draws upon scientific advance being part of the American origin story. This myth, partly true, is what has made the United States a very powerful nation. But myths are transferable (Turner 2013). Anything can be considered a 'frontier'. A big part of the myth is that the frontier is empty and waiting to be discovered, so it runs against the myth to dwell on the collateral damage that frontier conquest has brought about. Indian Removal, fake land claims from the Treaty of Guadalupe Hidalgo and the immorality of the Atlantic slave trade complicate the myth in politically fraught ways (Turner 2013).

But what if 'the frontier' is us? Turner (2013) uses an example of a company that is making a ski cap with sensors in it that can collect neural data and, with the help of AI, read the wearer's mind. The 'frontier' mentality is such that the legitimate question regarding why we should pursue this particular frontier never really gets addressed or adequately debated. The algorithmic contract involves the affording of legitimacy to 'tech explorers' to discover, innovate, and provide us with 'new lives' free from anxieties and regrets.

It is telling that many of the computer scientists that make social media tools have been distancing themselves (and their families) from these products. Many Silicon Valley tech workers send their children to schools where iPhones, iPads, and even laptops are banned. The Stanford psychologist BJ Fogg (2002) coined the term 'captology' to define the ways in which technologies can be designed to impact opinions, attitudes, and behaviours. Captology has been applied in a myriad of ways to develop tech tools designed to capture our attention (Harris 2016). Tech companies and product designers have become remarkably skilled at using the psychological needs and tendencies of users to capture attention. Social media, combined with mobile phones, may indeed be the perfect devices for 'pushing our inner buttons'.

For instance, Facebook's algorithm ranks changes to profile pictures higher and moves them up individual feeds because social praise – likes and comments – keeps people on the site longer (Harris 2016). Members of cohesive communities tend to receive higher levels of social praise and connection than those in more diffuse communities. Social media tries to group people based on homophily, or shared beliefs and interests, reinforcing these bonds. This desire for praise creates a cycle: we get praise from people with shared beliefs and interests, which is rewarding, so we seek more people with shared beliefs and interests in the hopes that they will give us more praise. Tech companies aid in this by constantly suggesting new accounts for us to follow. The more connections we have, the more potential mutual obligations we form. This web of responsibilities keeps us on the site longer.

Tech companies use intermittent variable rewards to maintain user engagement. Slot machines generate more revenue in the United States than baseball, movies, and theme parks combined. People become addicted to slot machines three to four times faster than other games (Dow Schüll 2012). This is why social media apps have a scroll function like that of a slot machine. This reward system activates the limbic system when we feel we are missing out on something critical for our survival. Constantly checking social media gives the illusion of relieving 'FOMO' (fear of missing out), but in reality, it often heightens anxiety. Posts that provoke controversial or emotionally charged reactions intensify FOMO by creating a sense of threat or by reinforcing solidarity, making them more successful in capturing attention.

Another tactic used by platforms is the concept of 'bottomless bowls' (Harris 2016). Research shows that people eat 73 per cent more when given a bottomless bowl of soup, underestimating their consumption by 140 calories (Wansink 2011, 6). This is why YouTube auto-plays the next video by default – it provides the illusion of there being no scarcity. It gives the user a permission structure to continue consuming content by creating the illusion of endless choice.

Human nature is not easily predictable, nor can it be entirely controlled by algorithms. Just as dominant personalities emerged in 1970s communes to disrupt egalitarian harmony, algorithms today can lead to homogenized, superficial engagement, stifling intellectual growth. The promise of a transcendental 'new life', implied in the algorithmic contract, paradoxically exposes us to algorithmic tools that undermine our efforts at 'knowing ourselves' – in ways counter to the view of the Romantics. If the aim of these technologies is to make us more predictable, what happens to those who seek to resist this predictability? How can we coexist with technologies that push for optimization while at the expense of individuality?

Algorithms and the promise of order

The algorithmic contract promises the allure of orderliness via optimization and classification. Orderliness brings the belief in greater safety, which presumably alleviates anxiety. While we want to relieve anxiety, we also want to connect with the world as it is, even if that world is sometimes chaotic and unpredictable. The transcendentalist counter to the algorithmic contract resonates in our society. It is why a common reaction to someone being 'too online' is to 'touch grass' in the vein of Thoreau's nature walk.

Touching grass, taken seriously, is a challenge to the dictates of technocapitalism. A 'non-datafied' subject is an underused resource from the perspective of a data broker. It is an 'untapped oil well' in the language of Toonders (2014). We are currently in a middle position where the serenity of our offline, tactile lives is threatened by social media and digital platforms, but not entirely replaced. Instead, we live in a space between the analogue and digital. But for how long?

In *The Question Concerning Technology*, Heidegger (2009) argued that technology 'uproots man', noting that human relationships are fundamentally technical. Technology invites us to reveal ourselves through our engagement with and transformation of nature. For Heidegger, modern technology transforms objects, turning them into resources to be extracted and studied, rather than experienced in their being. The tree becomes nothing more than a source of potential energy or raw material for extraction. In today's data-driven world, we speak of 'data extraction' and 'data mining', revealing humans to be just another stock of resources to be optimized for the dictates of technocapitalism. When everything is viewed through the lens of optimization, human relationships and experiences that resist such quantification pose a challenge. These elements defy optimization precisely because their value lies in time, friction, and unpredictability. There seems to be a desire to return to this analogue world, but as Heidegger suggests, once technology has brought into being a way of seeing the object, we can never truly return to how it was before.

But if Heidegger is right, are we in an irreversible 'optimization age' where our ability to tap into our 'divine spark' and 'remain algorithmic problems' is diminished? Have we become commodities who are more valuable as part of market clusters and have become habituated to prefer the order and security of classification? Have the tools of algorithmic classification 'brought into being' selves that are forever trapped in a 'machine habitus' – a set of dispositions for thinking algorithmically in ways that reinforce categorization and drive us to crave the 'algorithmic order' of abstraction/classification at the expense of uncertainty (Airoldi 2021)?

The Austrian writer Heimito von Doderer used the word *anschauung* to describe an unfiltered experience of reality, free from abstraction, analysis, or mediation (von Doderer in Hren 2022). This unmediated existence is integrative, intuitive, and holistic. *Anschauung* is an ideal state, perhaps akin to the Buddhist Nirvana, but the further we stray from *anschauung* towards algorithmic abstraction, the less we are able to empathize with others. For von Doderer, the artist's purpose is restore a sense of *anschauung* against the forces of abstraction (von Doderer in Hren 2022). The decline in attention spans brought about by the shift to video social media platforms is linked to a decline in experiencing a 'sense of presence'. Novels require work – they require the reader to immerse themselves in a world, to be present to it. In an algorithmic classification society, the concept of *anschauung* becomes increasingly remote, exacerbating the problem of the outlier for those who seek unfiltered experiences outside of prescribed classifications, potentially limiting their ability to make autonomous decisions based on holistic understanding rather than algorithmic categorizations. We evaluate literature, the arts, the classics through an optimization and classification lens, asking 'does this fit my current model?' rather than 'what can I learn about engaging with this work?'

Optimized selves struggle to deal with the inherent contingency of the world – loss, grief, illness, and so on. In his writing, von Doderer often referenced *fatologie*, a concept from Thomas Aquinas that involves accepting 'the role life exacts' (Hren 2022). This embrace of one's fate, of accepting oneself as one is, with all one's limitations and potential, and following the path that fate portends, is the antithesis of the algorithmic contract. The aimless meandering involved in following that path completely is undoubtedly sub-optimal. It can be winding, aimless, and charming – like Joyce's *Ulysses* or a prog rock song with a 10-minute harpsichord solo. These artistic projects mirror the twists and turns of life. The concept of *fatologie* is also antithetical to the algorithmic contract. Accepting one's fate conflicts with the 'new life' project the algorithmic contract promises.

The life of the mind teaches us to embrace the mystery of the world, finding beauty in what we cannot fully comprehend. But it also invokes terror and dread. Labatut (2021, 187) describes the sense of vertigo we experience from living in a world where we use tools whose inner workings we do not fully understand:

> We know how to use it, it works as if by some strange miracle, and yet there is not a human soul, alive or dead, who actually gets it. The mind cannot come to grips with its paradoxes and contradictions. It's as if the theory had fallen to earth from another planet, and we simply scamper around it like apes, toying and playing with it, but with no true understanding.

But the algorithmic contract does not present our engagement with technology through the lens of relieving anxiety. It prioritizes the possibility of novelty, discovery, and distraction through online life. We can understand the world through engagement with online tools. But wisdom requires sub-optimal, sustained engagement. The dopamine hit of the TikTok scroll provides more immediate payoff than the contingent and laborious cultivation of long-term relationships or the intermitted payoff of reading a long meandering novel.

Emerson (1841, 30) writes in 'Self-reliance' that 'man is his own star', suggesting that each person contains elements of the divine. But the emphasis on that passage is about 'capacity'. Our Internet age ignores that part of transcendentalism that advises reflection in nature to find the inner spark, instead offering us a synthetic version of the world at our disposal where we can find an optimal 'to become' self. It is easy to misinterpret our algorithmically curated environments as 'our spark'.

In the ordinal society, the outlier is the one who reflects upon and challenges their algorithmic categorization. However, ours is an age of deep institutional scepticism. The 'orderliness' that would seem to come about through algorithmic classification is not producing an orderly society. This is understandable when we think of what the algorithmic contract proposes. Why succumb to an authority figure when you can gather information yourself? We can see this reaction to institutions all around us. As a college professor for over 20 years, I have observed a gradual increased reluctance among students to read material for its intrinsic value. This is a good example of the effects of optimization culture on humans. Professors cannot assign reading for the sake of reading and reasonably expect that students will read it. As a professor, students may think that I do not really have anything of value to give them because what I know about political life can presumably be gleaned from Wikipedia or 'Internet research'. As a result, many students will only read what connects to the test, which makes reading instrumental.

Rather than 'becoming' into themselves, they are closing off those avenues in exchange for the safe classification of the algorithm.

Optimization culture has led to a loss of confidence in scientific validity and a flattening in the quality of knowledge claims. Today, it has become fashionable to tell people to 'do their own research'. But this 'research' often consists of Googling online, gathering evidence about various aspects of life. The Internet, particularly platforms like YouTube and social media, has made the research process much more accessible and widespread, transforming the tools of discovery and dissemination into everyday instruments for many. How do we make sense of when someone like popular podcaster Joe Rogan claims to have done 'research' to substantiate anti-vaccine claims (Bond 2022)? On one hand, his is an 'outlier position' that forces scientists to vet their claims in the court of public opinion. But information searches are not conducted in a neutral, good-faith information environment. They are the product of predictable algorithmic curation. The perception of an autonomous subject searching for their 'inner compass' gets distorted by algorithmic control that shapes the content of all information searches. This produces a culture where users are flattered into believing they have found their 'inner spark' even if they lack good-faith neutral information search capabilities, the training to understand scientific research, and the space for reflection needed to apply it towards useful ends. In March of 2024, the *Washington Post* reported on an increase in viral TikTok videos offering misinformation regarding birth control. One TikTok video showing a woman cutting up her birth control pills garnered over a million likes, reflecting a growing trend of social media posts that blame the pill for severe side effects and encourage women to stop using it (Weber and Malhi 2024).

This part of the algorithmic contract taps into our strong desire, at least in the US context, to 'master ourselves' independent of formal institutions or authority. The power of the mind and will to overcome challenges has been a central tenet of many influential thinkers and self-help gurus in the United States. It favours 'possibilitarians' who are always optimistic (Peale 1952). This mentality is exemplified by figures like Steve Jobs, Bill Gates, Elon Musk, and Jeff Bezos, who have presumably pushed the boundaries of human achievement. The algorithmic contract offers this vast range of 'tools of self-mastery', coupled with a global 'hustle culture' that equates worth with work. The results are much less rosy. Few online influencers make a profit – 'hustle culture' predictably leaves most of us exhausted, cynical, and frustrated, which we can then express online in our own algorithmically curated ways.

Instead of self-improvement, we have the opposite. There are multiple crises occurring simultaneously in Western societies – a crisis of liberal democracy, a crisis of capitalism, a youth mental health crisis, a rural 'deaths of despair' crisis, a 'crises of young men', and so on. This, I suggest, is because the algorithmic contract is producing *nihilists* rather than genuine sceptics. True scepticism, which often drives deep reflection, does not drive social media engagement. Algorithms reward sensationalism and polarization, which can lead to ideological entrenchment. In many ways, Kierkegaard's (1841) differentiation between cleverness and wisdom in *The Concept of Irony* offers insight here. Cleverness is performative, often used to avoid confronting the absurdities of life, while wisdom embraces the unknown. Algorithms, in their optimization, often foster cleverness as a means to generate quick, engaging content – but they seldom encourage wisdom. Kierkegaard viewed cleverness as part of an inferior life to the aesthetic and the ethical, whereas true wisdom, for him, involved embracing the absurd and the suffering that comes with human existence. This performative cleverness, often rewarded by algorithms, can devolve into self-deception, avoiding the deeper engagement needed to cultivate genuine wisdom – an essential element of functioning democratic societies.

Burnout and the algorithmic contract

The most pernicious effect of the algorithmic contract is to replace our innate human search to live in a world of *things* and replaces it with non-things intended to relieve our anxiety through distractions or comfort (Han 2022). According to Han, the world of things is messy and imperfect, yet has a layered, multitudinal quality, like von Doderer's *anschauung*. Analogue music, for example, becomes a 'thing' not just by being a physical object like vinyl, but through the full range of sound it produces, including the dirtiness of clicks and pops from the debris in the grooves. This imperfection gives vinyl its 'mystery'. Things, because they are not abstracted, do not immediately convey meaning or reveal themselves; their purpose is not to communicate clear meaning or to be 'optimal' (Han 2022). Like humans (things), who as Whitman (1855) famously noted, 'contain multitudes', things are not reducible to a singular meaning. On the other hand, online data is a 'non-thing' because it lacks a layered, multitudinal quality. It is not designed to convey meaning, to uncover multitudes slowly, but to quickly disseminate *information* for neoliberal consumption or power acquisition (Han 2022). While a narrative, such as in a novel, is complex and opaque, data is smooth, transparent, and packaged for consumption. Data is meant to encourage mindless consumption, but it lacks its own essence.

The algorithmic contract prioritizes information over narrative. Narrative is sub-optimal. Layers take time and energy to peek back, time that could be spent consuming. Han (2022) wants us to move us away from the transactional transparency of the information society toward the complexity and mystery of art. For example, Han claims a poem is a 'thing' because its value cannot be reduced to a single interpretation. But we cannot embrace the complex and mysterious because we are 'always engaged' in a digital life that instils impulsivity, affect-based communication, and excessive consumerism (Han 2022). By removing spaces for reflection, the digital world robs us of the necessary environments to experience awe and respect. Han (2022) uses the concept of radiation to emphasize how the analogue world allows interplay between light and shadow, in contrast to the digital world, which pushes us towards rigid profiles rather than allowing our identities to emerge from complex, analogue experiences.

This nuanced understanding of human experience is something the 'machine habitus' is blind to, as it is solely engaged with the process of optimization towards the local minima, not with the development of ourselves separate from the 'we'. Freedom from domination is about having control over one's experience. To be autonomous is to live in a world that provides individuals with tools to create a fully functioning self that is separate from the algorithmic cluster, not detached from the community, but from the world of 'non-things' that remove us from the human experience. Without this ability, we risk falling into unquestioning collectivism or totalitarian conformity because we prioritize comfort and distraction over life. The distraction of the algorithmic contract ultimately leads to a form of *affliction* – the soul-sucking experience of not being able to give meaning to one's own suffering (Weil 2023).

Lured by the promise of the algorithmic contract, we slowly descend the feature hyperplane towards a truncated, abstracted self that represents a fractional version of what we might have otherwise become. We are turned into obsessive 'brands' that, as Byung-Chul Han (2022) notes, are engaged in providing users with 'non-things', marketing ploys that communicate *information* with no texture or nuance. While many tech companies are concerned with UX and human-centred design, much of this is oriented towards turning full subjects into abstracted brands, rather than reducing affliction. This is evident in how algorithms keep us engaged: they are intimately concerned with optimizing the amount of engagement on social media, without any abiding interest in the quality of that engagement.

This is because spaces for true individuation, however, often conflict with the needs of market capitalism. This is a core aspect of the algorithmic contract: the abandoning of the process of classifying ourselves and ceding that responsibility to the algorithm. This means giving up on using 'similitude' to construct our identities (Foucault 1970). Similitude is central to the knowledge-creation process in modernity, allowing us to draw analogies and see similarities and differences between things. Thinking by analogy is a natural part of human cognition, but the algorithmic contract undermines this natural process of similitude. In the pre-algorithmic world, similitude was something we actively sought out. It was a transparent process: we knew who was engaging in the language game of similitude. Art was a way we could transmit representations to others. With algorithms, we are limited in our ability to reflect on and act upon the connections presented to us.

The algorithmic contract encourages us to see ourselves as empowered through the algorithmic contract, as if we are pursuing a romanticized view of the world, guided by our Emersonian 'inner spark' to see the beauty around us. Relying on our sense of control and autonomy, we mistake the abstract world seen through devices for the messier, more pluralistic real world. The more this abstraction is pointed out, the more algorithmic citizens grow distrustful of institutions. This perspective is alluring. Being able to portray oneself as the anachronistic 'truth-teller' with 'secret knowledge' that sets one apart from the 'sheeple' is a compelling and powerful narrative. It offers a life lived inwardly, subjectively, and untouched by 'corrupted' institutions and places one in the tradition of the grand historical revolutionaries of the world.

Yet, the myth of the isolated romantic is just that. The original 18th-century Romantics in the United States and Europe were not passive observers of life. The German Romantics of the 18th and 19th centuries interweaved their rich 'inner emotional lives' with social experiences such as wine-fuelled dinner parties and letter exchanges (Wulf 2022). Theirs was a dialogic, not isolated, existence, which contrasts sharply with today's digital consumption of endless videos and online content. Liberal democracies are never going to meet this ideal of a nation of *bon vivants*, nor should we want that. But there needs to be a critical mass of 'culture makers' that break out of their algorithmic classification to challenge the social order and remain algorithmic problems.

At its worst, performative cleverness can devolve into darker politics. There is a history of techno-romanticism turning into a flirtation with totalitarianism. Italian Futurists, a movement of the 1920s, associated technology with Italian fascism, because they claimed they both celebrated action and movement. Liberal democracy, by contrast, often struggles with decisive action. This leads to 'decisionism' – the will of the masses, frustrated by liberal democracies that seem slow to act because they value participation and input from diverse stakeholders (Schmitt 2007, XVII).

Decisionism and movement is wrapped up with the algorithmic contract's promise of a 'new life'. The consequence of this new abstracted, classified self is an insistence that the abstracted world becomes real. The move towards the local minima of one's classification is one that draws users closer to a desire for the abstracted world presented through the algorithm to be reflected in the real world. This desire produces a 'reactionary mindset', characterized by 'indignation' (a sense of victimhood and a call to action), 'decadence' (a motif that posits the present as morally corrupt and harkens back to a more virtuous golden age), and 'conspiracy' (the identification of hidden enemies or plots that are concealing truth) (Shorten 2021, 21–25).

All three trends are clearly evident throughout our online lives, amplified by the algorithmic contract.

Reaction can lead to totalitarianism. Totalitarianism arises when masses who have been 'uprooted' begin to exhibit 'startling novelty' and superfluousness (or statelessness) (Arendt 1951). Arendt thought solitude was important for democratic citizens because it gave individuals the ability to contemplate and reflect. Loneliness and isolation, however, were different than solitude. Under loneliness, people feel misunderstood and isolated from their fellow citizens. They start to question themselves and everything around them. When citizens are isolated, they are more vulnerable to totalitarianism. In totalitarianism, ideology pervades citizens in such an all-encompassing way that there is no distinction between public and private life.

The algorithmic contract relies on our isolation. An isolated self is a more optimal product for classification and consumption. But this comes with profound externalities. The 'isolated individual is vulnerable to being mobilized to a new loyalty' (Arendt in Wilkinson 2010, 51). Isolation makes individuals susceptible to someone or something that provides the missing bonds of community – something that can create a sense of belonging. This is a thin belonging, motivated by repeated exposure to 'non-things' (Han 2022). If enough individuals are exposed to the same non-things, they can be prompted to escape into a predictable and comprehensible 'unreality' that is abstracted from the world and may provide comfort but also undermines the values of pluralism and liberal democracy.

This is the ultimate danger of the abstraction that the algorithmic contract presents. It gives the user a sense of comfort and 'freedom from choosing' that, if sufficiently detached from the physical world, turns individuals with diverse, cross-cutting communities and interests into 'masses' that want to impose their abstracted version of the world upon reality. Although not written during the age of the algorithm, Arendt's (1951, 351) observations are applicable today. Arendt observed that a people detached from social life become vulnerable to a demagogue that can provide them with meaning and purpose, however fantastical the stories told to support that meaning and purpose might be. Once 'the masses' become convinced that they are tasked with upholding that meaning and purpose, they are prone to 'want victory and success as such, in their most abstract form ... [M]ore important than the cause that may be victorious ... is the victory no matter what cause, and success no matter what enterprise'.

The 'stability' of the abstracted self becomes a new, more concrete identity. Arendt (1951, 365) notes how 'Nazi propaganda was ingenious enough to transform antisemitism into a principle of self-definition, and thus to eliminate it from fluctuations of mere opinion'. By 'self-definition', she meant that propaganda gave 'the masses of atomized, undefinable, unstable and futile individuals a means of self-definition and identification which not only restored some of the self-respect they had formerly derived from their function in society, but also created a kind of spurious stability' (Arendt 1951, 341–2). While the algorithmic contract is not specifically designed to promote totalitarian propaganda, it does not distinguish between those self-definitions that lead to totalitarianism and those that only promote lifestyle consumption.

The masses' escape from reality is a verdict against the world 'out there', which does not satisfy their need to belong or construct meaning. The algorithmic contract does not provide users with appealing terms if economic, social, and political systems are satisfying their needs. Human beings need meaning-making institutions to make sense of a chaotic world. The 'commodification of everything' (Marcuse 1964) undermines the transformation of chaotic and accidental conditions into a man-made pattern of relative consistency. In the absence of a social order that is meaningful, individuals become vulnerable to propaganda: '[W]hat convinces the masses are not facts, and not even invented facts, but only the consistency of the system of which they are presumably a part ... Totalitarian propaganda thrives on this escape from reality into fiction, from coincidence into consistency' (Arendt 1951, 130).

The corrolary to the reactionary, authoritarian mindset is that the algorithmic contract discourages the development of independent thought, a seeking out of idiosyncratic novelty and a penchant for creative expression. The Internet is transforming into a place of numbness, filled with rote performances and sterile interactions (Kriss 2022). Far from its reputation as a source of creativity, it has become a 'low-resolution reality' filled with graven images of people and things that lack value (Kriss 2022). This is the flipside of the reactionary mind, and algorithmic conformity (the move towards the local minima) seeks *amplification* over discovery. The engagement algorithm reinforces users' synthetic, abstracted worldview hundreds of thousands of times. A tour of a social media feed will see familiar tropes of 'outrage clips' of a candidate or a surrogate doing something to 'troll' the opposition, usually in uncreative ways which echo other similar clips. Novelty becomes subordinate to mundane amplification in ways that appear 'zombified'. I am always struck by my few forays into Instagram or TikTok: scrolling mindlessly through amusing or enraging videos inevitably has a numbing effect on my psyche.

This zombifying numbness is our desire to be unburdened from the responsibility of civic life, a form of 'quiet quitting' of civil society. To flourish and reach the 'ideal form' of oneself, individuals need 'political freedom' or an environment that supports collective action and participation in public affairs. This perspective suggests policies that foster community engagement, public spaces, and participatory governance. This world where anomaly detection and algorithmic control shape the ways we interact, both politically and socially, is not one where we 'account for ourselves'. It is one where we allow the algorithm to abstract us to avoid the complex and fraught work of public life. The irony is that the abuse and criticism we receive in our mediated spaces are likely more piercing than the critiques we would receive if we engaged in political action. But we nonetheless resign ourselves to our mediated spaces.

The allure of social media, at one point, was the ability to 'argue for your existence' on a public platform (Siegel 2022, 19). This is slightly different than Arendt's (2013 [1958], 57–58) call to deliberate over and act upon the world we *share in common,* or as she put it 'to live together in the world means essentially that a world of things is between those who have it in common, as a table is located between those who sit around it; the world, like every in-between, relates and separates men at the same time'. While both are important, the algorithmic contract emphasizes the importance of the former over the latter. Social media has undeniably provided people with tools to 'assert their existence', if not argue for it. This taps into a fundamental instinct that 'flows from our intuitive certainty that our right to exist is the most fundamental truth, and that our right to exist is bound up with our freedom to think about existence in specific ways' (Siegel 2022, 34).

Arguing 'for our existence' (Siegel 2022, 14) on social media creates a recursive loop: we argue for our existence at time point 't', but algorithms condition and shape how we are heard, which in turn has an ontological impact on how we exist (and how we should exist). We subsequently adjust the ways we 'argue for our algorithmically mediated existence' at time point t+1, based on the feedback we receive from others (which is also algorithmically mediated). Because existence is not static, there is not a fixed point from which we argue. Instead, algorithmically mediated existence evolves dialectically (or cybernetically). We 'argue for our existence' on social media because we want our unique individual existence to be recognized. But to be recognized, we make adjustments to fit the dictates of the algorithm, which move us incrementally towards our classification (towards the local minima). Whatever our initial efforts at 'arguing for our existence', they become lost or distorted in this process.

Factory farming analogy

A useful metaphor for thinking about the unintended consequences of the algorithmic contract is our experience in the United States with factory farming. Like farm animals raised in controlled environments for predictable and profitable outcomes, our behaviours and decisions are increasingly shaped by algorithms that prioritize efficiency and profitability. However, just as factory farming has unintended consequences – such as antibiotic overuse, poor feed, and environmental degradation – so too does our growing reliance on algorithms, as they steer us towards predictable patterns of thought and action.

A dilemma of human existence is how to consume enough calories to not only meet basic nutritional needs, but to thrive. Animal protein is a nutrient-dense source of calories and nutrients, but historically animals are hard to reliably kill, store, and consume. This problem in the last century has been solved in much of the world. To satisfy our insatiable craving for meat we have created a very efficient and brutal system of factory farming.

Over the last few decades, the US meat diet has shifted from diverse sources to primarily chicken, driven by campaigns positioning chicken as healthier and cheaper. Centralization in factory farms, where only a handful of facilities raise millions of chickens, mirrors the monopolization of data collection and processing by a few tech giants. Industrial farming practices have significant public health and environmental impacts caused by intensive corn and soy farming for livestock feed.

In the United States, the process of raising and consuming beef has multiple stages, due to a lack of competition in the industry. From the small-scale rancher that raises calves from birth, to a background ranch, to a feed lot that 'finishes calves' and sells them to a meatpacker who then sells them to a distributor supermarket. At these final two stages the industry becomes remarkably concentrated; as with other industries, a push for deregulation in the 1980s led to a significant consolidation of meatpackers such that there are only a handful of major players who set the terms for price and process (Bult 2021).

To optimize this system, however, producers have to find ways to reduce risk. In the United States, market competition makes it such that growers compete, not simply to produce meat, but to do so in ways that are appealing to customers, by injecting animals full of hormones to 'plump up' animals for consumption. Additionally, this system produces a great deal of waste that needs to be disposed of. Food & Water Watch (2023) estimates that dairy farms in the United States tend 2 million cows that produce 85 billion pounds of manure annually. Waste from dairy and hog farms, as another example, are often stored in lagoons that flood and overflow during storms, spreading nitrogen and phosphorous into nearby fields and waterways. This excess of nitrogen and phosphorous feed algae and sparks toxic blooms that harm marine life and humans if the blooms get into municipal water systems.

The mega factory farm industry in the United States is built upon managing the risks associated with mass-scale industrial farming. This produces an ethically questionable treatment of animals, as if they were an inanimate consumer product. It is a strange paradox that we have an infinite capacity for sympathy towards individual animals – our pets for instance – but lose this compassion when we ponder the massive scale of industrial farming.

For example, the meat industry breeds far more animals than will be slaughtered as a hedge against disease and injury (Splitter 2021).

The adoption of 'mega factory farms' offers insight into how centralization reshapes both agricultural and digital worlds. The economic implications are stark: smaller farms are squeezed out, just as smaller voices are drowned in the digital noise. This outsourcing of control has unintended consequences, much like the environmental costs of biofuel subsidies that convert grasslands into fuel crops. The factory farming industry is an example of a solution to the optimization problem. Optimizing for affordable animal protein consumption has created serious environmental and health externalities, but as it stands, there is an unspoken contract between suppliers and consumers. As an analogy, it allows us to think about the ways our relationships to consumer society and the algorithms that increasingly govern them creates unintended consequences. Industrial farming changes the relationship between producer and consumer, subject and object. Similarly, when humans relinquish control over critical processes to algorithms, the subject and object relationship changes – we lose the capacity for reflection and understanding.

This factory farming analogy becomes even more pressing in the age of generative AI. Philosophical arguments, such as John Searle's (1980) 'Chinese room' thought experiment, suggest that while AI can process information, it lacks true comprehension. As AI technologies advance, the risks of automating human thought processes without proper oversight become more apparent. We become our own 'Chinese room problem', engaging in behaviour without the reflective apparatus to know why we are behaving as we are. We are operating on the assumption that if something can be automated, it should be, but this mindset overlooks the unintended consequences of algorithmic control, such as the loss of 'free-range', independent thought. In contrast to factory-farmed citizens, those who think in metaphor and engage in diverse language games retain their capacity for creativity and nuance. The metaphor of the 'spherical cow', used in machine learning to describe oversimplified models, warns us against reducing human experience to predictable patterns. The spherical cow refers to the tendency of scientists to reduce a problem to the simplest form imaginable to make calculations feasible. The phrase references a joke about the danger of substituting the abstract for the real:

> Milk production at a dairy farm was low, so the farmer wrote to the local university, asking for help from academia. A multidisciplinary team of professors was assembled, headed by a theoretical physicist, and two weeks of intensive on-site investigation took place. The scholars then returned to the university, notebooks crammed with data, where the task of writing the report was left to the team leader. Shortly thereafter the physicist returned to the farm, saying to the farmer,

'I have the solution, but it works only in the case of spherical cows in a vacuum.' (Lee 2013)

As we navigate the algorithmic age, we must remain vigilant against becoming 'farmed citizens' whose actions are driven by abstraction rather than individuality and public action. More importantly, we need to recognize our complicity in our algorithmic abstraction. Animal rights ethicists use the Marxist distinction between exchange and use value, counterposing the market price of an animal's meat against the intrinsic value of the animal as a living being. To eat meat requires a 'wilful ignorance' towards how animals are being raised. To stay in the algorithmic contract as it is currently constructed requires a similar wilful ignorance. What would the terms of a renegotiated algorithmic contract look like? I will expand upon this in the next chapter.

7

Algorithmic Obligation

Our optimization culture poses a paradox. We believe we have free will and are autonomous agents, yet many feel a sense of unease, almost as if we are being programmed but do not quite know how or by whom. Jack Dorsey (2024), the former CEO of Twitter, said as much at the Oslo Freedom Forum in 2024, noting that 'the free speech debate is a complete distraction' right now and suggesting that 'we are being programmed … through these [algorithmic] discovery mechanisms'.

We are immersed in a culture where we feed on an information diet produced exclusively for us based on a mixture of what we say we are interested in, which prompts the algorithms to find a cluster of like-minded others to serve us with content to keep us engaged. This incrementally sharpens the simplified 'pictures in our heads' that Walter Lippmann (1965) thought we used to organize our political lives.

An overarching concern with this book is the question of how humans *remain algorithmic problems* under the terms of an algorithmic contract that provides countless pressures to submit to algorithmic classification. Algorithms are designed to make users more predictable, improving daily in their ability to do so, while at the same time offering users the illusion of autonomy through a 'new abstracted identity' that relieves the anxiety of a messy, pluralistic world. Through optimization algorithms and vast troves of consumer data, companies have become more skilled at knowing our desires but are still unable to capture the full contingency of human experience. Predictability is crucial for marketers to increase click-through rates and for companies to demonstrate the effectiveness of their algorithmic models. I have suggested in this book that the 'problem of knowability' is addressed through an *algorithmic contract*. In exchange for the tools of information, entertainment, and voice (a freedom from boredom), users surrender their autonomy in curating this vast trove of content to engagement algorithms. They opt to 'relieve the burden of choosing' (Fisher 2022). If we cannot be predicted by algorithms, we can be made more predictable through the development of a 'machine habitus' (Airoldi 2021) that systematically moves us towards predictability, or much like a gradient descent algorithm progresses towards the local minima to reduce the cost function of our own abstracted optimization.

However, while algorithms aim to make users predictable, they simultaneously provide what appear to be tools for disruption, turning users into individual public storytellers within customized media ecosystems. This gives many users a feeling of empowerment and relevance. As Flisfeder (2021) notes, this disruption is largely symbolic and leads users to increased cynicism about institutions when their desires cannot be fulfilled by algorithms. This feeling of empowerment, however, serves as the basis of the algorithmic contract – we get what we want in exchange for endless distraction and the possibility of a 'new life' (Beer 2022). Platforms, in turn, are empowered to monetize this 'freedom' to enhance algorithmic predictability through extracting individualized, subjective data from users and steering them towards optimizing behaviour within their classification.

The wages of the algorithmic contract, however, are high. They serve to undermine our own individuality and our ability to perceive and protect the other as being worthy of dignity and respect. We develop a machine habitus to become 'optimizers' ourselves, scanning the environment to police conformity, identify anomalies, and relieve our anxieties about uncertainty. More importantly, it renders human subjects into commodities – much like animals that are factory farmed for consumption. Neoliberal capitalism, aided by platform capitalism, incentives users to 'cultivate voice' and to become an 'entrepreneur of oneself' (Han 2015) for the purpose of classifying/predicting subjects.

I liken this 'fencing in' of our epistemic potential to art critic Daniel Larkin's (2022) observation of how our imagination about Catholicism is tightly controlled by museum exhibitions. He conjectures that the Vatican, with its extensive collection of Old Master artworks, controls loans to galleries by setting strict terms for how the art can be displayed, to the effect, Larkin argues, of constraining the broad range of expressions of Catholicism. Larkin suggests that curators and museum directors tread carefully, sometimes even leaving out key facts and crucial observations in wall texts, press releases, and catalogues in which scholars are edited – or censored. Or, as he notes, 'as long as the Church is not offended, the loans will be delivered' (Larkin 2022).

Whether by design or not, this flattening of expressions of Catholicism ignores the plurality of ways to be. Ornate priest garments as 'queer' expressions are excluded from museums that want to maintain good relationships with the Church. Larkin begins his essay with the fact that few people know that Andy Warhol was a devout Catholic, something that would strike most people as surprising. Larkin (2022) notes: '[W]hat feels like the right way to write about Catholicism, or Christian iconography more broadly, to most art critics today is heavily influenced by the discourse they absorb at museums, which is far from neutral'.

The algorithmic contract produces a similar dynamic to the Catholic Church in this scenario. Our view of the world is dictated by an external agent, contorted to produce an abstraction that feels like reality. The algorithmic contract gives us what we want, and, in exchange, we become classifying subjects, constantly sorting experience via the lens of 'this belongs to that'. Religion belongs to right-wing reactionaries. Trans identity is code for permissive relativism. In reality, we are much more complex selves, but we become 'habituated' through recommender algorithms to behave predictably in ways that mitigate market risk/unpredictability in a 'technoliberal' world (Fish 2017). But pursuit of efficiency and optimization in a system can lead to unintended consequences and externalities, just like it does with factory-farmed animals (injection of hormones and antibiotics in animals, environmental degradation). For humans it means the loss of individuality, a lack of belief in liberal democracy, and a startling attraction to totalitarianism.

An algorithmic rights approach

Since the controversy over Cambridge Analytica in 2016, both tech companies, the press, watchdogs, and state actors have placed more urgency on educating the public on the issue of data rights. These critical issues have often been discussed under the liberal formulation of rights as individualistic and based on possession of property. Property rights in the United States are often discussed as a 'bundle of sticks' that include elements like possession, control of use of property, the ability to exclude others from using it, control over enjoyment of the object, and the rights of disposition (that is, inheritance) (Hohfeld 1913). The conventional understanding of data rights includes encompassing 'the rights individuals have over their personal data, empowering them to exercise control, privacy, and consent in the digital realm' (Shehu and Shehu 2003, 2). Legal frameworks like the EU General Data Protection Regulation and the California Consumer Privacy Act are built atop this 'bundle of rights' framework. In recent years, a 'data rights' framework has extended to questions of civil rights, that is, how data is used in decision-making and whether discriminatory algorithmic bias is being employed.

With the advent of AI and large language models, the debate about data sovereignty has shifted towards questions of infringement of copyrighted material used to train models and whether using this material to train AI represents an instance of fair use. Companies like Microsoft, Google, Apple, Twitter, and Meta all have their own sources of training data composed of proprietary data, but in each of these cases much of the training data involves vast amounts that is human-generated. The *New York Times*, among other entities, is suing OpenAI for using data scraped from its website to train its large language models (Roth 2023). Microsoft is also being sued by a group of programmers who claim that Microsoft trained its CodePilot using GitHub without the programmer's consent (Roth 2024). Finally, in 2023, a group of artists sued StableDiffusion for using their art without permission (Vincent 2023).

This individualistic formulation of 'data rights', while critically important, significantly constrains the ways in which data is used to undermine individual freedom. Data, like people, does not exist in a vacuum. There are broader dynamics that impact individual access to fundamental rights. To speak of rights solely in terms of non-interference from the state ignores the ways in which other factors can conspire to undermine liberty. A *social rights* approach includes, in addition to civil and political rights, a set of social rights such as 'the range of rights to welfare, security and to live the life of a civilized being according to the standards prevailing in the society … carried out through social institutions like the public education system' (Marshall 1964, 132). This broader set of rights speaks to the ethical imperative to uphold the dignity of individual human life. To speak of rights only as a 'bundle of sticks' that provide rules for how property can be used misses this broader point.

There is a serious question as to whether this atomized view of justice is applicable to the algorithmic age. As our lives become increasingly wrapped up with algorithms, a 'bundle of sticks' approach seems insufficient. Risse (2023) argues that because our epistemology is being impacted by algorithms, they should be included in a theory of rights. We have shifted from an analogue lifeworld to a digital lifeworld, but we have not properly theorized what this means for justice and human rights (Risse 2023).

Risse merges the Kantian view of 'humans as ends' with the concept of epistemic injustice (Fricker 2007). Epistemic injustice deals with the ways in which the lived experience of individuals from different groups is discounted, either in the form of denying the credibility of their testimony or excluding individuals from a society's meaning-making processes and thus the language to discuss their experience. Epistemic rights include protecting individuals as knowers (producers of knowledge) and knowns (subjects of knowledge) (Risse 2023). The threat of algorithms for Risse is their ability to engage in epistemic intrusiveness through algorithmic curation. Subjects should be seen as people with 'epistemic actorhood', not simply as passive vectors of data suitable only for data extraction. He defines an epistemic actor as a 'person or entity integrated into some communication network – some system of information exchange – as seeker or revealer of information' (Risse 2021, 3).

What would an epistemic rights framework do to the algorithmic contract? While Risse's framework is an important advance in its focus on epistemic rights, I want to propose that algorithms also have obligations to users not just to protect their epistemic rights, but to develop their epistemic capacities and potentialities. Algorithms should not violate the epistemic rights of users by devaluing their narratives or experiences by placing them lower in their recommendation rankings. This is a starting point. But algorithms also need to ensure that users have a right to 'grow' and 'become' in ways that preserve their autonomy without truncating their potentialities.

Embedded in this expanded notion of a right is Risse's identification of the subject as a *knower*. The subject's epistemic rights, in such a case, must extend beyond simply access to whatever information the algorithm chooses to provide. It should include a right that broadens one's epistemic capacity. Instead of seeking universal answers, algorithms should be obligated to emphasize democratic pluralism and diverse narratives. This constitutes something of a 'right to be epistemologically challenged'. Yet, the algorithms driving our online interactions are not programmed for this kind of intellectual humility because they do not contribute to platform engagement.

Part of a renegotiation of an algorithmic contract includes a right to not have our potentialities limited by optimization algorithms. Algorithms should be obligated to contribute to a user's development of a rewarding and meaningful life. That does not mean simply reflecting life as it is or steering it towards an optimized point for consumption. Rather, algorithms should promote meaningful encounters in digital place/space. In 'The Right to the City', Henri Lefebvre (1996) relies heavily on philosophy and art to serve as guideposts for how individuals can claim a 'right to place', highlighting the particularities of art to unify and reveal the totality of urban life.

In the context of data, this means developing a *right to algorithms* that encourage a sense of play, exploration, and creativity, rather than merely optimization and control. In 'The Right to the City', Lefebvre (1996) is careful to point out that the urban form of a city points to, but does not determine, social interaction in cities. The urban form may encourage residents to live in more rigid and uniform ways than they otherwise would, or it could empower them to live meaningful, fulfilling lives, but communities have their own specific cultural and social 'way of life'. Here, he introduces the idea of an 'urban fabric' – the network of relationships that play out within a given urban form. The urban fabric can be thought of as the interaction between urban form and the lived experience within communities. An example he uses is that the urban fabric of pre-industrial societies before zoning laws (distinct residential and commercial districts) encouraged habitats with more 'plasticity', or the ability to modify the use of space to meet one's needs (Lefebvre 1996, 94). Imbuing algorithms with a sense of play means recognizing and respecting the complexity and depth of human experience and creating spaces and systems that support and nurture that experience (and foster its growth), rather than reducing and constraining it for the purposes of neoliberal capitalism.

The idea of making online spaces available for play rather than acquiescing to the 'seriousness' of optimization/anomaly detection is not as far-fetched a proposition as one might suppose. Our current social media landscape has multiple spaces where individuals experience a sense of play. TikTok and Instagram are filled with creativity and encounter. But a precondition of play is a sense of trust. If creativity and encounter is used to demean, marginalize, or diminish, then the platform is not protecting the epistemic rights of its users. This is regrettably often the case on social media platforms that feign neutrality on posts that demean and marginalize others. This, even if done in a comedic or clever way, is the opposite of play. If the broader question of play is about self-determination and autonomy and being in a community of co-creation, then it is hard for a true sense of play to occur when algorithms promote content that demeans others.

One example of an entity that fosters a sense of play is the presence of a handful of free-form college radio stations in the United States. In the late 1990s, I briefly attended the University of North Carolina at Chapel Hill. Its radio station, WXYC, was a free-form station that had a rule where the DJs could not play music from any genre twice in the same hour. This both forced the DJ to stretch their musical knowledge and produced a sublime musical education for a twenty-something music lover. Thirty years later, I will still turn the station on to expose myself to new music not recommended to me based on my prior tastes, but completely orthogonal to what I have previously liked. There are so few free-form radio stations in the United States because they are 'sub-optimal'. One might have to wade through several songs and genres one does not like to get to a song one enjoys. Why go through the trial of enduring what you may not like? Algorithms have the potential to habituate us away from familiarity and more towards the epistemological resilience and openness needed for human flourishing. Three principles should guide this: an ability to capitalize on serendipity, a right to synthetic potentiality, and a cultivation of Boolean fuzziness.

A right to serendipity

Part of developing one's epistemological capacities is to have the preparation necessary to take advantage of serendipity. As Olma (2016, 14) points out, 'the search for new knowledge is a sheer impossibility as one either knows what to look for, in which case the object of the search is not new, or one doesn't know what to look for, which makes the search impossible'. Serendipity is not a synonym for luck. In its original meaning, serendipity is more akin to acquiring the wisdom, insight, and preparation necessary to recognize and capitalize on unexpected events (Olma 2016). *Serendipity* is the 'wisdom and discernment that enable individuals to make judicious decisions and connect the dots in a meaningful way' (Olma 2016, 23–5).

Insight involves perceiving underlying patterns and understanding the deeper implications of information or situations. *Preparation* means cultivating the knowledge, skills, and mental readiness that position one to take advantage of unforeseen opportunities.

These three attributes are not simply about seeking out novelty, but about cultivating the habits that allow you to derive meaning and value from serendipitous moments. Olma describes Alexander Fleming's discovery of penicillin as a confluence of chance (accidental contamination of a bacterial culture) and serendipity (the ability to recognize the applications of the accidental combinations in killing bacteria). Without his training as a bacteriologist, Fleming would have been unable to capitalize on his accidental discovery (Olma 2016, 30–2).

The history of science reveals a 'serendipity pattern' as central to knowledge creation (Merton and Barber 2004). Rather than be the anomalous instance of an otherwise predictable and orderly pattern of scientific discovery, serendipity was central to the process of many scientific discoveries. The narrative of scientific discovery, however, downplays the role of accident. For much of modern history, science has been rooted in positivism, a philosophy where scientists strive to create overarching 'covering laws' that explain how the world works. They develop theories about these workings and empirically test them, using hypotheses to guide their observations. In this view, truth emerges from observing the 'knowable world' and building a general body of knowledge that explains it (Merton and Barber 2004).

This is not the way we typically think science works. The fundamental aim of science is to contribute to a broader body of knowledge by producing new insights. This endeavour is grounded in the principles of the scientific method, which involves systematic observation, experimentation, and hypothesis-testing to build and verify knowledge. What we choose to observe and how we choose to set up experiments are rooted in our cultural contexts. The scientific approach downplays this reality, ignoring the role that other ways of knowing such as folk wisdom, intuition, or even faith play in the knowledge production process.

But including serendipity into scientific analysis changes our underlying assumptions. Olma discusses the concept of *poiesis*, a concept described in Plato's 'Symposium' as the process of something coming into being. This is distinct from Aristotle's praxis, emphasizing that poiesis has an end beyond itself, resulting in the generation of something novel. The idea of 'bringing an idea into being' connotes some divine or mystical origin. Indeed, the ancient Greeks tied scientific discovery to the pursuit of divine knowledge. This is a very different way of viewing scientific discovery than the scientific method we all learned as teenagers (Olma 2016).

Risse (2023) calls for access to education as part of his formulation of epistemic rights. However, it is important to specify what kind of education fosters and sustains epistemic rights. Risse lays out the distinction between different ways of knowing. Empiricists argue that knowledge comes exclusively from observing the real world, as opposed to intellectual reasoning about it – an approach rooted in the work of Francis Bacon. Auguste Comte observed that theory and observation were interconnected, with theories needing to be verified through observation (*positivism*). The move towards empiricism and positivism separated science from serendipity. *Interpretivism*, or *antipositivism*, asserts that because observation is subjective and historically/contextually situated, groups of people will interpret the world in different ways. What truly matters is what things mean to people, rather than some externally existing 'truth'. From this perspective, there exists a plurality of 'ways of seeing', or *epistemes*, that are rooted in power relations.

Optimization algorithms can do damage by structuring the meaning-making process for individuals such that their experience of the world is so abstracted as to bear little resemblance to reality. The result is that arriving at a sense of epistemic integrity becomes impossible. In the hypothetical scenario of someone who adopts a Marxist and/or postcolonialist world view, their episteme might be one that sees the world through class relations or colonizer/colonized relationships. If that view is reinforced by algorithms that amplify the message then our hypothetical subject may be led to believe that their epistemic mission is to uncover hidden structures of oppression and domination that are often obscured from view. In this hypothetical, it is proper to say that this person's epistemic rights have been preserved, but have their epistemological capacities been developed? Have they held their beliefs up to critical or empirical scrutiny? It is possible they have, but this is not a given. Another example might be ethnonationalists or religious extremists that adopt a rigid orthodoxy that allows them to posit all sorts of external threats as rooted in reality such that everything is filtered through the orthodoxy of what preserves their 'in-group'. The algorithmic contract gives the hypothetical ethnonationalists the option of preserving their epistemological rigidity rather than fostering their sense of epistemological capacity.

A right to serendipity tracks with having the epistemic flexibility to see possibilities, to leverage serendipity. The Berkeley philosopher Paul Feyerabend, in *Against Method*, advocated for a 'counterinductive' science that emphasizes a flexibility of mind by proposing that researchers speculate and build testable theories and hypothesis on 'the opposite' of what they thought to be true (Feyerabend 1975). For this kind of epistemic flexibility to be useful, we must have institutional structures that allow individuals to capitalize on their innovative capacities.

Back in the late 2000s, Olma observed that our innovative infrastructures are not conducive to promoting the generative accidents necessary for serendipity to occur. This is even more true today. Our current environment includes many new technologies like the Metaverse, Web3, and cryptocurrency that are unlikely to lead to significant advances in technology and commercial innovation. Funk et al (2022) argue that the reason for this is the de-emphasizing of basic research and development at private companies, leading to universities as the primary locus of research.

> The biggest change from that era is the decline of basic and applied research at companies. Until the 1970s, most of this research was done at corporate laboratories such as Bell Labs, RCA, and DuPont, research that led to both Nobel Prizes and real products and services such as transistors, integrated circuits, plastics, and radar.

They argue that challenges of the culture of academia – a perish or publish system of tenure, hyper-specialization, disincentives for applied research, and so on – make it difficult to translate basic research to market innovation. The publish or perish mindset makes it difficult to be counter-inductive. Science advances less through discovery and more through the development of research programmes (Kuhn 1970). Junior scholars are not in the position to go against a research programme, lest they lose funding and a network of mentors should they challenge orthodoxy. The practice of science today is riddled with overtures towards conformity. The issues of confirmability raise concerns about whether measurements are accurate or whether fraud is involved. The repeatability or reliability of findings is another area of concern, highlighted by the problem of p-hacking (the manipulation of statistical model components so as to produce statistical significance and hence inflate their explanatory power). Finally, there is the question of whether research stands up to peer review, a concern that touches on the replication crisis currently facing modern science.

Our algorithmic lives bear similarity to the culture of academic publishing. With the proliferation of 'influencers' and 'brand builders' online, the culture of classification makes users less practiced at capitalizing on serendipity, instead using their creative possibility to reinforce brand maintenance – in much the same way that graduate students and junior scholars much defend 'research programmes'. Indeed, scholars on social media platforms bear little resemblance to their scholarly selves, indulging in un-rigorous thought to attract followers. True serendipity requires spaces where individuals are encouraged to take risks, to be 'counter-inductive'. Our algorithmic environment is set up to make users optimization machines that see risks as 'anomalies' rather than remaining open to serendipity.

Some suggestions for introducing unpredictability include using 1) algorithms to introduce 'randomness', using natural language processing (NLP), 2) give a 'bias score' to threads/closing down or randomizing those that exceed a given score, and 3) having a 'random' option to randomize newsfeeds and Twitter streams. But this unpredictability is bound to lead to less engagement. People might hate the discomfort of the algorithm adopting an obligation to extend their epistemological capacities. This is the core challenge of renegotiating the algorithmic contract – we like our algorithmic optimization and do not want the discomfort of having it changed. It is more comfortable for us to be unreflectively ideological than to have epistemological humility and flexibility.

A right to digital potentiality

Related to the idea of serendipity is a right to be exposed to novelty associated with a sense of play. Without opportunities to engage with the unexpected, we cannot evolve as individuals. Our modern technoliberal environment inhibits play. A recent example is the 'scandal' that resulted from Google's roll-out of its Gemini AI image generator in early 2024. Users of the new AI found that it seemed to be 'erroneous' in the images it produced. For example, a recent *Vox* article reported on a user that asked Gemini to draw an image of a Pope and rather than get a Western white male, Gemini drew a female pope of Indian origin and a black-phenotyped pope. Similarly, asking Gemini to draw a Nazi resulted in an implausible multicultural tableau of SS officers (Samuel 2024).

The vast majority of observers saw this as a calamitous rollout for Google's Gemini, so much so that the company shut down the image generator to the public. One conservative analyst referred to it as Google's 'Bud Light moment', referencing that company's promotional video with a popular transgender social media influencer (Dumas 2024). The perception was that Google had erred in its efforts to overcorrect racial ethnic Western bias in its training data. In its efforts to be 'politically correct', it failed to be 'truthful' in its depictions. The inability to present 'things as they are' caused shareholder handwringing, but few stop to ask why should it be the role of any AI to always be truthful? Using Lefevre's language, what is so wrong about allowing an image AI to introduce as sense of 'play' or 'possibility' into its images? What exactly is so wrong about using an AI to synthetically depict a Black pope?

One useful way to look at Google's 'woke AI' is to see it as generating possibilities – as providing the marginalized with the opportunities to envision possibilities. Martel (2017) coins the term 'misinterpellation' to describe ways in which social change can occur. Misinterpellation expands on Althusser's (2006) theory of interpellation where subjects are constituted by those in power through 'calls' or 'hails' that only certain groups are expected to answer. Althusser uses the example of a police officer calling out 'hey, you' to someone on the street. When someone turns around, they accept that they are the subject of the call. In a broader sense, a call dictates who is invited to adopt certain roles and identities and who is excluded from them. Martel proposes the radical possibilities of marginalized groups *misinterpellating* or responding to 'calls' that were not actually intended for them. This is different than Risse's view of epistemic recognition – it is a right to make a claim to an episteme from which one is presumably excluded. Martel argues that misinterpellation is not a mistake, but a potentially revolutionary act. It highlights how marginalized people can take seriously universal discourses of rights, freedom, and democracy in ways not intended by those in power. This suggests a 'right to potentiality', or to 'misinterpret' a call and hence to resist power and reimagine political subjectivity.

An AI that 'hallucinates' is also one that helps us envision a world of possibilities rather than simply give us back an 'accurate' representation of reality (something we do not always need AI to do). Algorithms have the obligation to uphold the principle of 'synthetic potentiality'. Theorizing the synthetic gives us a way into thinking about how we police the deployment of imagination through technology. The discourse regarding Gemini's 'hallucination' never became subject to debate. It was a given that people would be outraged about Gemini producing unconventional images because they did not reflect the reality of history. This, I suggest, is because tech companies' preference is for optimization. Hallucination is automatically seen as sub-optimal and should be eliminated. A 'hallucinating' AI can provide us with an additional means of exploring 'who we are' that can supplement, not replace, community.

The point is not to invalidate the critique that any image AI should have some level of historical accuracy. Drawing diversity into all historical settings can also serve as erasure of histories of racial discrimination and oppression. But at the same time, imbuing an AI with a sense of 'play' or 'whimsy' can provide the possibility of imagining difference in ways that could point to a more open, pluralistic society, and ultimately what Lefebvre (1996, 73) referred to as a 'society as an oeuvre' (work of art).

I liken this obligation to potentiality to what Chappell (2022) calls a 'republic of conversation' – a community of open dialogue and diverse perspectives constituted by members with an epistemological humility fostered through remaining open to 'epiphanies' (Chappell 2002, VII) – transformative experiences that challenge established ways of being. This requires the rejection of systematic theories – of the impulse to optimize. Instead, Chappell highlights the cultivation of 'wow' moments through fostering the imagination.

Algorithms are inherently complex and as such are always going to involve some degree of illegibility. Human decisions are always embedded within algorithms. If we accept this as a given, we can advocate for a more expansive algorithmic obligation. Amoore (2020) refers to the ways in which algorithms can produce new identities and formulations as 'fabulation'.

She defines fabulation as the ways in which algorithms 'invent a people' through a 'curious body of correlated attributes' (Amoore 2020, 98–9). Rather than reject this constructed reality, however, Amoore suggests we engage with it, by recognizing the fabricated nature of algorithmic outputs, seeing them as avenues for possibility rather than finalized, optimized outputs. A 'cloud ethics', for Amoore (2020, 102), requires insisting on the complex, pluralistic nature of humanity and resisting the 'resistant terrain of the unattributable' (that is, the algorithm's ability to arrive at decisions without understanding or human accountability).

Algorithms have the veneer of certitude, but Amoore (2020) insists on maintaining a sense of 'undecidability' about whether ground truth can ever approximate actual truth. Features and attributes in transformer models are fundamentally abstractions, and, as such, can change and are subject to being constituted differently; what Gillespie (2014, 1888) calls 'calculated publics'. As humans, our attributes are socially derived (a 'society of attributes'), which evolve and change over time (Amoore 2020, 155–57). All algorithms miss key attributes in its classification of subjects. Because of this, we need to keep open the idea that decisions can lead to alternative pathways not envisioned by the system, viewing the algorithm as the 'field of meaning' that produces spaces in which we operate, not final decisions (Amoore 2020, 156).

Rather than relying on a hypothesis-testing approach, we may benefit more from adopting a descriptive or hypothesis-generating perspective on scientific problems. If not, we risk going around in circles. By structuring our choices algorithmically, recommendation algorithms encourage us to close off those avenues that would explain us differently or predict different futures for us. The algorithmic contract is an exercise in reduction – in narrowing possibilities for us, reducing our chances of knowing what those different futures might look like. Making an algorithm transparent is insufficient.

Algorithms intervene in the phenomenology of our world. We are not just presented with different options based on the parameters and weights of a model; our experience (and our ideas about the world) also changes. This organizing of the world through data and machine learning creates a system that depends upon those abstractions and supports them through the logic of optimization where the imperative is 'accuracy'. There are obvious moments where accuracy is paramount. We would hate structural engineers to abandon accuracy when calculating beam loads to explore 'potentialities' in real time.

But human existence is not an optimization problem; in some ways we can think of it as a *de-optimization* problem of gathering the wisdom to know that the world is sub-optimal, full of beauty, sorrow, and possibility. Oscar Wilde (1923, 63) remarked in his essay 'The Decay of Lying' that lying, 'the telling of beautiful untrue things', is the proper aim of art. Wilde feared the decay of literature due to society's obsession with representing things as they are. He warned that if we fail to check our worship of facts (or optimization), ' and beauty will pass away from the land' (Wilde 1923, 15). Art is a corrective to the algorithm which 'tells untrue things' but does so in a reductivist, abstracted way that narrows one's experience of the world. Wilde's call is to embrace possibility through the exploration of the sublime.

Similarly, Kurt Vonnegut (1998) introduced the concept of 'foma' – 'harmless untruths' – in his novel *Cat's Cradle*. One of the more quoted passages from that novel goes, 'Live by the foma that make you brave and kind and healthy and happy' (Vonnegut 1998, VII). This idea encourages us to live by the stories and beliefs that enrich our lives, even if this conflicts with the world as it is. A right to epistemic capability is the ability to engage with algorithms that help one evolve in one's life journey – to share and listen to the experience of others and to not be pigeonholed into 'defending one's narrative' or challenging another's 'harmless untruths'.

Boolean fuzzy citizenship

Part of a renewed algorithmic contract should also include the development of AI and algorithmic tools that promote *fuzziness*. The idea of fuzziness comes from the insight among some scientists that we should move beyond rigid classifications popular in inferential statistics that insist on identifying universal causal variables. The fuzzy alternative would move us towards 'set theory' methods that highlight the diverse ways that social phenomena occur (Ragin 2000). Put simply, instead of seeking 'universal explanations', a Boolean approach suggests identifying the various causal pathways to the dependent variable. This approach proposes linking independent variables into 'Boolean chains' of causality to find combinations of conditions that lead to specific outcomes. Fuzziness then adds an additional layer of nuance through the insight that individuals are not binary in their categorization, but rather probabilistic.

The value of a Boolean approach for social sciences is to emphasize the plurality of context-dependent ways that phenomena exist in the world. This means AI outputs that provide Boolean chains of possibility rather than singular answers to queries. But Ragin (2000) observed that the utility of a Boolean approach was limited by its use of binary or categorical variables, what is often called 'crisp set' Boolean analysis. Fuzzy sets, by contrast, allow for more nuanced analysis by allowing membership in a category to fall between 0 and 1. A fuzzy method recognizes the reality that few people or cases ever falls squarely into a '0' or '1' binary.

This is not just a methodological difference but an ontological one. Fuzzy-set methodology rejects binary thinking, allowing for more nuanced understanding of category membership. Those who deploy algorithms have an ethical obligation to contribute to fuzzy-set over crisp-set thinking. This responsibility involves using algorithms that expose citizens to 'orthogonal perspectives' – viewpoints that are related to their fuzzy set membership but not 'crisply' optimized. This means transforming binary or categorical data into fuzzy probabilities. Recommendation algorithms that base their output on fuzzy classification rather than crisp sets promise users a broader, multifaceted worldview.

A binary 'optimization' logic towards individuals runs the risk of abstracting users in dangerous ways. A binary mentality is also one that is absolutist and inflexible regarding compromise. Fuzziness suggests seeing users as having membership in multiple categories simultaneously. An algorithm that optimizes for 'fuzziness' would emphasize a kind of 'homoeostasis' where users are not algorithmically pushed into one category or another but are balanced among the multiple categories of which they are a full or partial member.

With the advancements in NLP, particularly through transformer and attention models, algorithms can, and should, be trained to present users with 'possibilities' rather than merely giving them direct answers. This shift is essential because citizens conditioned to 'get what they want, when they want it' are at risk of being willing to sacrifice liberal principles and individual rights in exchange for the certainty and immediate gratification that the algorithmic contract currently provides. Instead of reinforcing dualistic thinking, the digital landscape can foster 'fuzzy citizens': individuals who engage with ambiguity and complexity, embracing uncertainty rather than seeking out definitive answers.

Koening-Archibugi (2012) uses the concept of 'fuzzy citizenship' to challenge binary notions of nation state membership. This view is based on the principle that anyone affected by government decisions should have the right to participate in that government, to reimagine a broader notion of citizenship. Fuzziness introduces the idea that citizenship is not binary but exists in degrees. This model would allow us to have 'stages' of citizenship. Some might not be full citizens, but if they are affected by state decisions, they could be granted partial citizenship that bestows some of the rights of citizenship, but not all, commensurate with the degree to which state actions impact their lives.

The idea of 'fuzzy citizens' recognizes that citizens in a democracy are not always neatly divided into rigid categories but instead may have overlapping, evolving, and sometimes contradictory loyalties and opinions. Promoting this kind of flexibility in digital spaces is essential for fostering democratic resilience, as it encourages individuals to resist binary thinking and engage in deeper, more nuanced forms of political participation. Social media platforms, through carefully designed algorithms, could play a crucial role in cultivating this mindset, thereby contributing to healthier democratic systems.

A fuzzy citizenship perspective has the potential to produce creative citizens who can use art and narrative to effectively advocate for desired goals. Liberal democracy is constantly in a process of needing to maintain its legitimacy. This requires creative forms of 'collective enchantment' through the creative development of fictions and fantasies that 'give life' to democratic ideals (Frank 2021, 134–35). In particular, Frank (2021, 3) argues, 'the people' is an imagined concept that requires aesthetic imagination: 'At the heart of modern democracy's fantasy space lies its enigmatic constituent subject: the people. Unlike the king ... the people that are the living source of democratic authority are never visible; the sovereign voice proclaimed in the revolutionary slogan vox populi, vox dei is never distinctly audible'. A fuzzy algorithmic approach exposes the user to a broader range of ways of being. Ceding curational authority to an algorithm designed to optimize us towards a classification orients us away from developing the kind of creativity needed for us to imagine 'democracy' and 'the people' in creative ways. We are more likely to think in 'crisp set' terms – in group versus out-group. There is a sense in which algorithmic classification can be tyrannical because it encourages us to become binary in our epistemology. Epistemological certitude, on most things, is counter to the democratic project. Having the epistemological humility to not fixate on a specific worldview is frightening for many, but necessary for democratic health.

Extraordinary politics

There is no shortage of ideas about how to reform algorithms, but many of these proposals presume a one-way process where platforms can change their algorithms, and the public will readily accept. The reality, as I have illustrated throughout this book, is that we are complicit in our algorithmic thinking. This is why it is useful to see our algorithmic age through the lens of a social contract. This contract, like any social contract, includes the prospect of exit or renegotiation. But what would that look like?

Kalyvas (2008, 6–12) argues that the founding moments of a democracy, 'the politics of the extraordinary', are crucial for granting legitimacy to democratic procedures. Democratic legitimacy stems from the 'founding moments' (Kalyvas 2008, 7). Kalyvas is critical of the two main ideological perspectives of modernity, Marxism and liberalism, for not addressing how 'new beginnings' happen in democratic life (Kalyvas 2008, 256–59). Classical literature focused more on the mythical nature of 'foundings' rather than their legalistic basis. As a result, we dismiss the idea of 'extraordinary moments' in liberal thought because they appear irrational, undemocratic and illiberal. But without a recognition of the 'extraordinary politics' that ultimately evolve into the normal constitutional politics, there is the risk of fuelling a crisis of democratic legitimacy with little prospect for meaningful democratic change. An emphasis on the extraordinary allows for a return to collective autonomy by making citizens the authors of their own rules and social life. Kalyvas (2008, 2) notes how social contracts come after the founding moments to legitimate them: 'The idea of a social contract was predominantly used to explain political obligation, to justify obedience, to describe the consensual basis of authority, and, in a few cases, to legitimate resistance, rather than to account for those historical moments of genuine rupture and transformation'. Kalyvas draws on Negri's (1999) distinction between constituent and constituted power. Constituted power (*potere*) is the static institutional power that upholds the social order, while constituent power (*potenza*) is the creative, dynamic force of democratic innovation: the possibility for changing the social order. *Potenza* is a spontaneous, creative, and boundless potential that exists for political transformation. Negri sees modernity as an ongoing confrontation between constituent and constituted power. The usefulness of Negri's approach is to see democracy as a perpetual process of self-creation, rather than as a static fixed set of institutions or processes.

Democracy is not a safe practice. Wolin (1994) sees democracy as innately 'transgressive', in that its default state is to challenge established political forms and norms. What distinguishes democracy is its revolutionary potential that holds out the possibility of disrupting and reshaping political orders. For Wolin, democracy is always 'in motion', resisting final, static institutional rule. In this way, he calls democracy 'fugitive', in that it always presents a danger to 'constitutional democracy', which he sees as attenuating rather than amplifying democratic impulses and is always trying to keep from being institutionally captured.

Each of these authors point to the transformational potential embedded within democracy. Kalyvas points to the need to see founding moments as 'extraordinary moments' in liberal democracy where significant transformational change occurs. This is echoed by Negri's emphasis on constituents' power to challenge systems and Wolin's view of democracy as uniquely transgressive. A change to the algorithmic contract requires users to take up their constituent power and demand radical change in how algorithms are deployed. This requires constant imagination in reframing and rearticulating the ways in which algorithms are deployed to reduce our humanity. Users need to see their relationship to algorithms as 'in motion' through engaging in acts of 'everyday resistance' against algorithmic domination using 'tactical algorithmic agency' (Bonini and Trere 2024, 4). As Bonini and Trere (2024, 19) write, there are many examples of this agency:

> Instagram 'pods,' Uber 'surge clubs,' attempts to fake personal workout loads and boost restaurant ratings, 'Tinder scams,' and 'spoofing' of

location-based videogames are just some of the dozens of algorithm gaming practices enacted every day by gig workers, fans, activists, and institutions of various kinds to make the algorithms work to their own advantage.

Each of these examples are efforts to reclaim agency from the algorithm. In two examples, Bonini and Trere (2024, 50) identify the practices of musicians gaming the algorithm to get their music heard by shortening the intro and putting choruses at the beginning of songs and Airbnb hosts using subtle methods to ensure they receive five star ratings from users. They detail more elaborate strategies to hack algorithms, like politicians using troll farms to increase engagement and popularity on a social media platform, the mass-scale generation of fake reviews on sites like TripAdvisor, and Uber drivers collaborating to manipulate the surge pricing algorithm to raise costs (Bonini and Trere 2024, 53–4).

Regardless of the algorithmic contract's tendency to reduce individual agency, humans in a liberal democracy always retain a 'fugitive' status – an ability to be transgressive and retain *potenza*, always retain agency to challenge the legitimacy of the current algorithmic contract. The assumption, as Bonini and Trere (2024, 4) note, is that users are in an asymmetrical relationship with platforms. Systemic change to the system that requires significant coordination to employ strategies of 'algorithmic sabotage' highlights the unfairness and indignity of the current arrangement. To go beyond everyday resistance requires not just 'gaming the algorithm' but an engagement with the political.

One such engagement with the political occurred in 2020 when hundreds of students in England protested the algorithmically allocated assignment of grades that marked down poorer students (the Ofqual algorithm). The students adopted the rallying cry 'Fuck the algorithm', ultimately leading to a government U-turn on the practice (Amoore 2020).

These efforts are potentially the start of a moment of 'extraordinary politics' where users reclaim their autonomy and individuality back from the algorithm on a mass scale. This 'exit' is not guaranteed. There are significantly more people who are content enough with the current algorithmic contract to prefer it in its current state. A renegotiation of the algorithmic contract requires a revolutionary moment – one that does not see algorithmic refusal as the only option. Algorithmic tools, as I have argued in this chapter, can serve as the basis for greater epistemic capacity by enhancing potentialities and exposing users to serendipity that is orthogonal to their interests.

The seeds of a renegotiation of the algorithmic contract, however, begin with the systematic 'exit' from the current regime. This requires the individual equipped with the awareness necessary to know that they are being abstracted and classified and the fortitude to remain an algorithmic problem.

This means rejecting platforms that cater to you with the ultimate aim of classifying you and encouraging you to 'move toward the local minima'. Green shoots of resistance are emerging that emphasize the creation of new, algorithm-free platforms or prioritize returning to the *analogue world*. NPR reported on pi.fyi, a platform created by Tyler Bainbridge, a former Meta employee who quit the company and created an algorithm-free social media platform (Allyn 2024). Chayka (2024) notes a growing 'slow culture' movement where young people take steps to eliminate algorithms from their lives. He cites the return of blogs, the growth of email newsletters, and a resurgence in the popularity of vinyl records and bookstores as indications of dissatisfaction with algorithmic culture. In my own experience, my young adult recently purchased a 'dumb phone' to reduce their dependence on social media platforms.

This longing for an *analogue culture* is not a rejection of algorithms, it is a desire to renegotiate the terms of the algorithmic contract. Resistance to the ubiquity of algorithms in our lives stems from the desire to become free from an optimized, abstracted information environment where 'non-things' predominate (Han 2022). There is a growing sense that the algorithmic contract has failed to deliver on its promises. What a renewed contract would look like is a political question. I have sketched out three principles designed to restore full human autonomy and agency.

Inevitably, an 'exit' from the current algorithmic contract will ultimately require engagement with the state. It is an open question as to whether our growing scepticism with technoliberalism will lead to a revolt against the near monopoly power of tech platforms. In the United States, the growing lobbying influence and political engagement of tech billionaires signals that their political influence is growing, not diminishing. The ongoing fight to preserve one's 'inviolate personality' (Warren and Brandeis 1890) is fraught with challenges but it is the core fight for the future health of liberal democracy and human flourishing. It is the central question of our time whether you or I want to embrace our truncated, algorithmic identities or remain an algorithmic problem.

References

Airoldi, M. 2021. *Machine Habitus: Toward a Sociology of Algorithms*. Polity Press.

Al-Khalaf, R. 2023. Cashing in on the algorithm. *The Times*, 17 September. Available at: https://www.thetimes.com/article/cashing-in-on-the-algorithm-gktfqk5kl [Accessed 15 September 2025].

Allyn, B. 2024. 'Examining the growing movement against the algorithms that control our lives'. *NPR*, 6 February. Available at: https://www.npr.org/2024/02/06/1229405652/examining-the-growing-movement-against-the-algorithms-that-control-our-lives [Accessed 15 October 2024].

Althusser, L. 2006. Ideology and ideological state apparatuses (notes towards an investigation). In A. Sharma and A. Gupta (eds) *The Anthropology of the State: A Reader*. Blackwell Publishing, pp 86–98.

Amodei, D. 2024. Machines of loving grace. Available at: https://darioamodei.com/machines-of-loving-grace [Accessed 27 October 2024].

Amoore, L. 2020. *Cloud Ethics: Thresholds of Knowledge, Justice, and Power*. Duke University Press.

Anderson, B. 1983. *Imagined Communities: Reflections on the Origin and Spread of Nationalism*. Verso.

Andrejevic, M. 2019. *Automated Media*. Routledge Press.

Arendt, H. 1951. *The Origins of Totalitarianism*. Harcourt, Brace and Company.

Arendt, H. 1972. *Crises of the Republic: Lying in Politics, Civil Disobedience, Revolution*. Harcourt Brace Jovanovich.

Aristotle 1999. *Nicomachean Ethics*. Translated by T. Irwin. Hackett Publishing Company.

Appel R.E. and Matz S.C. 2021. Psychological targeting in the age of Big Data. In D. Wood, S.J. Read, P.D. Harms and A. Slaughter (eds) *Measuring and Modeling Persons and Situations*. Academic Press, pp 193–222.

Aradau, C. and Blanke, T. 2022. *Algorithmic Reason: The New Government of Self and Other*. Oxford University Press.

Ashby, W.R. 1956. *An Introduction to Cybernetics*. Chapman & Hall.

Azucar, D., Marengo, D. and Settanni, M. 2018. Predicting the Big 5 personality traits from digital footprints on social media: A meta-analysis. *Personality and Individual Differences*, 124, 150–9.

Bacher-Hicks, A. and de la Campa, E. 2020. Social costs of proactive policing: The impact of New York City's stop and frisk program on educational attainment. Working Paper. Cambridge, MA: Kennedy School of Government, Harvard University.

Bail, C. 2021. *Breaking the Social Media Prism: How to Make our Platforms Less Polarizing*. Princeton University Press.

Barsky, D. 2022. *Human Prehistory: Exploring the Past to Understand the Future*. Cambridge University Press.

Bataille, G. 2001. *The Unfinished System of Non-Knowledge*. University of Minnesota Press.

Baudrillard, J. 1981. *Simulacra and Simulation*. University of Michigan Press.

Beer, D. 2022. *The Tensions of Algorithmic Thinking: Automation, Intelligence and The Politics of Knowing*. Bristol University Press.

Benjamin, W. 2008 [1935]. *The Work of Art in the Age of Mechanical Reproduction*. Penguin UK.

Berlin, I. 2014. Two Concepts of Liberty. In D. Matravers, J. Pike and N. Warburton (eds) *Reading Political Philosophy: Machiavelli to Mill*. Routledge, pp 231–7.

Bhaimiya, S. 2024. Gen Z and millennials are increasingly 'doom spending': Here's what it is and how to stop it. *CNBC*, 23 September. Available at: https://www.cnbc.com/2024/09/23/young-people-are-doom-spending-heres-what-it-is-and-how-to-stop-it.html [Accessed 29 January 2025].

Black, J. 2023. Review of the book *Algorithmic Desire: Toward a New Structuralist Theory of Social Media*, by Matthew Flisfeder. *Postdigital Science and Education*, 6(2), 691–704.

Blog2Social. 2025. Monthly active users in social media. *Social Media Report 2025*, 11 March. https://www.blog2social.com/en/blog/monthly-active-users-in-social-media/ [Accessed 27 April 2025].

Bond, S. 2022. What the Joe Rogan podcast controversy says about the online misinformation ecosystem, [Audio] *NPR*, 21 January. Available at: https://www.npr.org/2022/01/21/1074202087/what-the-joe-rogan-podcast-controversy-says-about-the-online-misinformation-ecosystem [Accessed 29 April 2025].

Bonini, T. and Trere, E. 2024. *Algorithms of Resistance: The Everyday Fight against Platform Power*. MIT Press.

Borges, J.L. 1998. The Library of Babel. In A. Hurley (ed) *Jorge Luis Borges: Collected Fictions*. Viking, pp 112–118.

Brady, W.J., Jackson, J.C., Lindström, B. and Crockett, M.J. 2023. Algorithm-mediated social learning in online social networks. *Trends in Cognitive Sciences*, 27(10), 947–60.

Brockman, G. 2023. The inside story of ChatGPT's astonishing potential. [video] *TED*. Available at: https://www.ted.com/talks/greg_brockman_the_inside_story_of_chatgpt_s_astonishing_potential [Accessed 17 June 2025].

Brubaker, R. 2022. *Hyperconnectivity and its Discontents*. John Wiley & Sons.

Bundesrepublik Deutschland (2017) Network Enforcement Act (NetzDG). *Federal Law Gazette* p 3352, 1 September. Available at: https://www.gesetze-im-internet.de/netzdg/ [Accessed 25 January 2025].

Bult, L. 2021. How 4 companies control the beef industry. [video] *Vox*. Available at: https://www.vox.com/videos/2021/9/29/22700589/beef-industry-meat-production-future-perfect [Accessed 29 September 2024].

Calvano, E., Calzolari, G., Denicolo, V. and Pastorello, S. 2020. Artificial intelligence, algorithmic pricing, and collusion. *American Economic Review*, 110(10), 3267–97.

Chappell, S.G. 2022. Republics of conversation: The normativity of talk in Plato up to the Theaetetus. In D. Zucca (ed) *New Explorations in Plato's Theaetetus: Belief, Knowledge, Ontology, Reception*. Brill, pp 83–113.

Chayka, K. 2024. *Filterworld: How Algorithms Flattened Culture*. Knopf Doubleday.

Cheng, L. and Tanglis, M. 2024. Artificial intelligence lobbyists descend on Washington DC: An analysis of the state of lobbying on artificial-intelligence related issues. *Public Citizen*. Available at: https://www.citizen.org/article/artificial-intelligence-lobbyists-descend-on-washington-dc/ [Accessed 27 January 2025].

Chen, L., Mislove, A. and Wilson, C. 2016. An empirical analysis of algorithmic pricing on Amazon marketplace. In *WWW'16 Companion: Proceedings of the 25th International Conference on World Wide Web*, Association for Computing Machinery, pp 1339–49.

Cheney-Lippold, J. 2011. A new algorithmic identity: Soft biopolitics and the modulation of control. *Theory, Culture & Society*, 28(6), 164–81.

Chiodo, M. and Müller, D. 2023. Manifesto for the responsible development of mathematical works: A tool for practitioners and for management. Available at: https://arxiv.org/abs/2306.09131 [Accessed 12 July 2024].

Clear, J. 2018. *Atomic Habits: An Easy and Proven Way to Build Good Habits and Break Bad Ones*. Penguin.

Cochrane, T. 2021. *The Aesthetic Value of The World*. Oxford University Press.

Combs, C. 2024. Social media companies testifying before Congress tomorrow combined to spend $30 million on lobbying last year - and employed one lobbyist for roughly every four members of Congress. *Issue One*, 30 January. Available at: https://issueone.org/press/social-media-companies-testifying-before-congress-tomorrow-combined-to-spend-30-million-on-lobbying-last-year-and-employed-one-lobbyist-for-roughly-every-four-members-of-congress/ [Accessed 15 May 2024].

Cowdrick, E. 1927. The new economic gospel of consumption. *Industrial Management*, 74, 208.

Crain, M. 2021. *Profit Over Privacy: How Surveillance Advertising Conquered the Internet*. University of Minnesota Press.

Crawford, K. 2021. *Atlas of AI: Power, Politics, and the Planetary Costs of Artificial Intelligence.* Yale University Press.

Crockett, M.J. 2017. Moral outrage in the digital age. *Nature Human Behavior,* 1, 769–71.

Crunchbase. 2025. *The Crunchbase tech layoffs tracker.* Available at: https://news.crunchbase.com/startups/tech-layoffs/ [Accessed 23 April 2025].

Cummins, E. 2022. When algorithms promote self-harm, who is held responsible? *WIRED,* 14 October. Available at: https://www.wired.com/story/molly-russell-suicide-platforms-mental-health/ [Accessed 27 December 2024].

Czubik, A. 2016. 'The right to privacy' by S. Warren and L. Brandeis – the story of a scientific article in the United States. *Ad Americam. Journal of American Studies,* (17), 211–9.

Dahl, R.A. 1961. *Who Governs? Democracy and Power in an American City.* Yale University Press.

Dalla Riva, C. 2022. Decline of key changes in popular music. *FlowingData,* 22 November. Available at: https://flowingdata.com/2022/11/22/decline-of-key-changes-in-popular-music/ [Accessed 22 November 2022].

Dam, C., Hartmann, B.J., Brunk, K.H., Kim, B., Mizoroki, S., Frosh, P. and Shifman, L. 2024. Marketing the past: A literature review and future directions for researching retro, heritage, nostalgia, and vintage. *Journal of Marketing Management,* 40(9–10), pp 795–819.

Davis, J., Purves, D., Gilbert, J. and Sturm, S. 2022. Five ethical challenges facing data-driven policing. *AI and Ethics,* 2(1), pp 185–98.

Deleuze, G. 1992. Postscript on the societies of control. In I. Szeman and T. Kaposy (eds) *Cultural Theory: An Anthology.* Wiley-Blackwell, pp 139–42.

Deneen, P.J. 2019. *Why Liberalism Failed.* Yale University Press.

Diakopoulos, N. 2020. Accountability, Transparency, and Algorithms. In M.D. Dubber, F. Pasquale and S. Das (eds) *The Oxford Handbook of Ethics of AI.* Oxford University Press, pp 197–213.

Dick, P.K. 1996. *Do Androids Dream of Electric Sheep?* Ballantine.

Dickinson, K. 2022. The Japanese call this practice tsundoku, and it may provide lasting benefits. *Big Think,* 28 December. Available at: https://bigthink.com/neuropsych/do-i-own-too-many-books/ [Accessed 5 November 2024].

Dorsey, J. 2019. How Twitter shapes global public conversation: Jack Dorsey at TED2019. *TED Blog,* 16 April. Available at: https://blog.ted.com/how-twitter-shapes-global-public-conversation-jack-dorsey-speaks-at-ted2019/ [Accessed 25 October 2024].

Dorsey, J. 2024. Speech at the Oslo Freedom Forum. Available at: https://oslofreedomforum.com/talk/the-power-of-open-source/ [Accessed 5 November 2024].

Doucette, M.L., Green, C., Necci Dineen, J., Shapiro, D. and Raissian, K.M. 2021. Impact of ShotSpotter technology on firearm homicides and arrests among large metropolitan counties: A longitudinal analysis, 1999–2016. *Journal of Urban Health*, 98(5), 609–21.

Dow Schüll, N. 2012. *Addiction by Design: Machine Gambling in Las Vegas*. Princeton University Press.

Dumas, B. 2024. Is the Gemini fallout a 'Bud Light' moment for Google? *Fox Business*, 1 March. Available at: https://www.foxbusiness.com/technology/is-the-gemini-fallout-bud-light-moment-google [Accessed 20 September 2024].

Durkheim, É. 1951. *Suicide: A Study in Sociology*. Translated from the French. The Free Press.

Duran, G. 2024. The tech baron seeking to purge San Francisco of 'Blues'. *The New Republic*, 26 April. Available at: https://newrepublic.com/article/180487/balaji-srinivasan-network-state-plutocrat [Accessed 27 July 2024].

Eady, G., Paskhalis, T., Zilinsky, J., Bonneau, R., Nagler, J. and Tucker, J.A. 2023. Exposure to the Russian Internet Research Agency foreign influence campaign on Twitter in the 2016 US election and its relationship to attitudes and voting behavior. *Nature Communications*, 14(1), 62.

Egbert, S. and Mann, M. 2021. 'Discrimination in predictive policing: The (dangerous) myth of impartiality and the need for STS analysis. In A. Završnik and V. Badalič (eds) *Automating Crime Prevention, Surveillance, and Military Operations*. Cham: Springer International Publishing, pp 25–46.

Emerson, R.W. 1837. The American scholar. In C.E. Norton (ed) *The American Scholar, Self-Reliance, Compensation*. American Book Company, pp 21–46.

Emerson, R.W. 1841. Self-reliance. In *Essays: First Series*. Project Gutenberg.

Farrell, H. and Fourcade, M. 2023. The moral economy of high-tech modernism. *Daedalus*, 152(1), pp 225–35.

Ferriss, T. 2007. *The 4-Hour Workweek*. Harmony.

Ferriss, T. 2010. *The 4-Hour Body*. Random House.

Feyerabend, P. 1975. *Against Method: Outline of an Anarchistic Theory of Knowledge*. Verso.

Fish, A. 2017. *Technoliberalism and the End of Participatory Culture in the United States*. Springer.

Fisher, E. 2020. The ledger and the diary: Algorithmic knowledge and subjectivity. *Continuum: Journal of Media & Cultural Studies*, 34(3), 378–397.

Fisher, E. 2022. *Algorithms and Subjectivity: The Subversion of Critical Knowledge*. Routledge.

Flisfeder, M. 2021. *Algorithmic Desire: Toward a New Structuralist Theory of Social Media*. University of Minnesota Press.

Floridi, L. 2023. AI as agency without intelligence: On ChatGPT, large language models, and other generative models. *Philosophy & Technology*, 36(1), 15.

Fogg, B.J. 2002. *Persuasive Technology: Using Computers to Change What We Think and Do*. Morgan Kaufmann.

Food & Water Watch. 2023. The economic cost of food monopolies: The dirty dairy racket. Available at: https://www.foodandwaterwatch.org/wp-content/uploads/2023/01/RPT2_2301_EconomicCostofDairy-WEB.pdf [Accessed 15 May 2024].

Foucault, M. 1970. *The Order of Things: An Archaeology of the Human Sciences*. Translated by Alan Sheridan. Vintage Books.

Foucault, M. 1976. *The History of Sexuality, Vol. 1: An Introduction*. Vintage Books.

Fourcade, M. 2021. Ordinal citizenship. *The British Journal of Sociology*, 72(2), 154–73.

Fourcade, M. and Healy, K. 2017. Classification situations: Life-chances in the neoliberal era. *Historical Social Research/Historische Sozialforschung*, 23–51.

Fourcade, M. and Healy, K. 2024. *The Ordinal Society*. Harvard University Press.

Frank, J. 2021. *The Democratic Sublime: On Aesthetics and Popular Assembly*. Oxford University Press.

Fricker, M. 2017. Evolving concepts of epistemic injustice. In *The Routledge Handbook of Epistemic Injustice*. Routledge, pp 53–60.

Fuhrer, M. 2014. *American Dance: The Complete Illustrated History*. Voyageur Press.

Funk, J., Vinsel, L. and McConnell, P. 2022. Web3, the metaverse, and the lack of useful innovation. *American Affairs Journal*, 6(4). Available at: https://americanaffairsjournal.org/2022/11/web3-the-metaverse-and-the-lack-of-useful-innovation/ [Accessed 22 August 2024].

Garett, R., Lord, L.R. and Young, S.D. 2016. Associations between social media and cyberbullying: A review of the literature. *mHealth*, 2(46).

Gellman, B. 2023. Peter Thiel is taking a break from democracy. *The Atlantic*, 9 November. Available at: https://www.theatlantic.com/politics/archive/2023/11/peter-thiel-2024-election-politics-investing-life-views/675946/ [Accessed 10 June 2024].

Giddens, A. 1999. Elements of the theory of structuration. In A. Elliott (ed) *The Blackwell Reader in Contemporary Social Theory*. Wiley–Blackwell, pp 119–30.

Gillespie, T. 2014. *The Relevance of Algorithms*. MIT Press.

Gilliard, C. 2022. The rise of 'luxury surveillance'. *The Atlantic*, 18 October. Available at: https://www.theatlantic.com/technology/archive/2022/10/amazon-tracking-devices-surveillance-state/671772/ [Accessed 28 October 2024].

Gioia, T. 2022. Is old music killing new music? *The Honest Broker*. Available at: https://honest-broker.com/p/is-old-music-killing-new-music [Accessed 5 April 2024].

Gladwell, M. 2008. *Outliers: The Story of Success*. Little, Brown and Company.

Grove, J.V. 2019. *Savage Ecology: War and Geopolitics at the End of the World*. Duke University Press.

Grove, J. 2020. From geopolitics to geotechnics: Global futures in the shadow of automation, cunning machines, and human speciation. *International Relations*, 34(3), 432–55.

Guitchounts, G. 2021. Neuroscience's existential crisis. *Nautilus*, 27 October. Available at: https://nautil.us/neurosciences-existential-crisis-238334/ [Accessed 18 July 2024].

Hong, S. 2020. *Technologies of Speculation: The Limits of Knowledge in a Data-Driven Society*. New York University Press.

Hallinan, B. 2023. No judgment: Value optimization and the reinvention of reviewing on YouTube. *Journal of Computer-Mediated Communication*, 28(5).

Halpern, O. 2015. *Beautiful Data: A History of Vision and Reason Since 1945*. Duke University Press.

Halpern, O. and Mitchell, R. 2023. *The Smartness Mandate*. MIT Press.

Han, B.C. 2015. *The Burnout Society*. Stanford University Press.

Han, B-C. 2017. *In The Swarm: Digital Prospects*. MIT Press.

Han, B-C. 2022. *Non-things: Upheaval in the Lifeworld*. John Wiley and Sons.

Hao, K. 2021. The Facebook whistleblower says its algorithms are dangerous. Here's why. *MIT Technology Review*, 5 October. Available at: https://www.technologyreview.com/2021/10/05/1036519/facebook-whistleblower-frances-haugen-algorithms/ [Accessed 17 August 2024].

Harris, T. 2016. How technology is hijacking your mind – from a magician and Google design ethicist. *Thrive Global*, 18 May. Available at: https://medium.com/thrive-global/how-technology-hijacks-peoples-minds-from-a-magician-and-google-s-design-ethicist-56d62ef5edf3 [Accessed 22 August 2024].

Haskel, J. and Westlake, S. 2022. *Restarting the Future: How to Fix the Intangible Economy*. Princeton University Press.

Hayek, F.A. 2007. *The Road to Serfdom: Text and Documents – The Definitive Edition* (ed B. Caldwell). University of Chicago Press and Routledge.

Hayward, C. 2009. Power and identity: An essay on Amy Allen's politics of ourselves. *Journal of Power*, 2(1), 173–90.

Heidegger, M. 2009 [1954]. 'The question concerning technology'. In *Readings in the Philosophy of Technology*. Garland, pp 9–24.

Henderson, D.R. nd. Vilfredo Pareto. *The Concise Encyclopedia of Economics*. Available at: https://www.econlib.org/library/Enc/bios/Pareto.html [Accessed 28 April 2025].

Herder, J. 2019. The power of platforms: How biopolitical companies threaten democracy. *Public Seminar*, 25 January. Available at: https://publicseminar.org/essays/the-power-of-platforms/ [Accessed 12 June 2024].

Hobbes, T. 1967 [1651]. *Leviathan*, edited by W.G. Pogson Smith. Clarendon Press.

Hohfeld, W.N. 1913. Some fundamental legal conceptions as applied in judicial reasoning. *Yale Law Journal*, 16(23).

Hren, J. 2022. A cartography of redemption: On Heimito von Doderer's 'The Strudlhof Steps'. *Los Angeles Review of Books*, 29 September. Available at: https://lareviewofbooks.org/article/a-cartography-of-redemption-on-heimito-von-doderers-the-strudlhof-steps/ [Accessed 10 September 2024].

Huenemann, C. 2021. December 5. Riding an empty suit. *3 Quarks Daily*, 20 December. Available at: https://3quarksdaily.com/3quarksdaily/2021/12/riding-an-empty-suit.html [Accessed 25 April 2024].

Igo, S.E. 2020. *The Known Citizen: A History of Privacy in Modern America*. Harvard University Press.

Isaac, M. and Wakabayashi, D. 2017. Russian influence reached 126 million through Facebook alone. *The New York Times*, 30 October. Available at: https://www.nytimes.com/2017/10/30/technology/facebook-google-russia.html [Accessed 18 July 2024].

Jarow, O. 2022. How algorithms undermine consciousness. [podcast episode] *Musing Mind*. Available at: https://www.oshanjarow.com/podcasts/algorithms-consciousness-eran-fisher-subjectivity-ai [Accessed 22 August 2024].

Jenkins, H. 2017. What Ever Happened to the Promise of Participatory Television?: An Interview with Adam Fish (Part Three)', *Pop Junctions*, 3 May. Available at: https://henryjenkins.org/blog/2017/05/what-ever-happened-to-the-promise-of-participatory-television-an-interview-with-adam-fish-part-three.html [Accessed 29 July 2024].

Kalyvas, A. 2008. *Democracy and the Politics of the Extraordinary: Max Weber, Carl Schmitt, and Hannah Arendt*. Cambridge university press.

Kant, I. 2017. *Kant: The Metaphysics of Morals*. Cambridge University Press.

Kelly, S.M. 2023. Snapchat users freak out over AI bot that had a mind of its own. *CNN*, 16 August. Available at: https://www.cnn.com/2023/08/16/tech/snapchat-my-ai-chatbot-glitch/index.html [Accessed 25 September 2024].

Khalaf, A.M., Alubied, A.A., Khalaf, A.M. and Rifaey, A.A. 2023. The impact of social media on the mental health of adolescents and young adults: A systematic review. *Cureus*, 15(8). Available at: https://www.cureus.com/articles/124411-the-impact-of-social-media-on-the-mental-health-of-adolescents-and-young-adults-a-systematic-review [Accessed 10 May 2024].

Kierkegaard, S. 1841. The concept of irony, with continual reference to Socrates. *Project Gutenberg*. Available at: https://www.gutenberg.org/files/60333/60333-h/60333-h.htm [Accessed 29 January 2025].

Knibbs, T. 2022. Instagram keeps showing me children's tragedies. *Wired*, 5 July. Available at: https://www.wired.com/story/parents-sick-kids-social-media/ [Accessed 15 June 2024].

Koenig-Archibugi, M. 2012. Fuzzy citizenship in global society. *Journal of Political Philosophy*, 20(4), 456–80.

Korte, L. 2024. Zuckerberg says he regrets caving to White House pressure on content. *Politico*, 26 August. Available at: https://www.politico.com/news/2024/08/26/zuckerberg-meta-white-house-pressure-00176399 [Accessed 11 January 2025].

Kriss, S. 2022. The Internet is already over. *Numb at the Lodge*, 18 September. Available at: https://samkriss.substack.com/p/the-internet-is-already-over [Accessed 25 April 2024].

Koopman, C. 2015. The algorithm and the watchtower. *The New Inquiry*, 2 September. Available at: https://thenewinquiry.com/the-algorithm-and-the-watchtower/ [Accessed 12 June 2024].

Kozyrkov, K. 2022. Making friends with machine learning. [video] *YouTube*. Available at: https://www.youtube.com/watch?v=1vkb7BCMQd0 [Accessed 15 August 2024].

Kuhn, T.S. 1970. *The Structure of Scientific Revolutions* (2nd ed.). University of Chicago Press.

Kurzweil, R. 2005. *The Singularity is Near: When Humans Transcend Biology*. Penguin Books.

Labatut, B. 2021. *When We Cease to Understand the World*. Translated by A.N. West. New York Review Books.

Lacan, J. 1988. *The Seminar of Jacques Lacan, Book II: The Ego in Freud's Theory and in the Technique of Psychoanalysis 1954–1955*. Translated by S. Tomaselli. Cambridge University Press.

Laclau, E. and Mouffe, C. 2014. *Hegemony and Socialist Strategy: Towards a Radical Democratic Politics*. Verso Books.

Laney, D. 2001. 3D data management: Controlling data volume, velocity and variety. META Group Research Note 6.

Lanier, J. 2006. Digital Maoism: The hazards of the new online collectivism. *The Edge*, 29 May. Available at: https://www.edge.org/conversation/jaron_lanier-digital-maoism-the-hazards-of-the-new-online-collectivism [Accessed 20 September 2024].

Lantz, N. 1987. Review of the Personality Assessment System. *United States Central Intelligence Agency*. Available at: https://www.cia.gov/readingroom/docs/CIA-RDP96-00789R002200230001-2.pdf [Accessed 10 October 2024].

LaPalme, N. 2018. Michelle Carter and the curious case of causation: How to respond to a newly emerging class of suicide-related proceedings. *Boston University Law Review*, 98, 1443–65.

Larkin, D. 2022. The art world's Catholic problem. *Hyperallergic*, 27 November. Available at: https://hyperallergic.com/754744/the-art-worlds-catholic-problem/ [Accessed 25 August 2024].

Laterza, V. 2021. Could Cambridge Analytica have delivered Donald Trump's 2016 presidential victory? An anthropologist's look at big data and political campaigning. *Public Anthropologist*, 3(1), 119–47.

Lazer, D.M.J., Baum, M.A., Benkler, Y., Berinsky, A.J., Greenhill, K.M., Metzger, F., Nyhan, B., Pennycook, G., Rothschild, D., Schudson, M., Sloman, S., Sunstein, C., Thorson, E., Watts, D. and Zittrain, J. 2018. The science of fake news. *Science*, 359(6380), 1094–6.

Lee, T. 2013. The Coase Theorem is widely cited in economics. Ronald Coase hated it. *The Washington Post*, 13 Sept. https://www.washingtonpost.com/news/wonk/wp/2013/09/04/the-coase-theorem-is-widely-cited-in-economics-ronald-coase-hated-it/ [Accessed 17 November 2024].

Lefebvre, H. 1996. The Right to the City. In E. Kofman and E. Lebas (eds) *Writings on Cities*. Translated by E. Kofman and E. Lebas. Blackwell, pp 63–184.

Levenson, J.C., Shensa, A., Sidani, J.E., Colditz, J.B. and Primack, B.A. 2017. Social media use before bed and sleep disturbance among young adults in the united states: A nationally representative study. *Sleep*, 40(9).

Levitt, H. 2024. JPMorgan's says every new hire will get training for AI. *Bloomberg*, 20 May. Available at: https://www.bloomberg.com/news/articles/2024-05-20/jpmorgan-s-erdoes-says-every-new-hire-will-get-training-for-ai [Accessed 22 May 2024].

Li, W.Y. 2023. Regulatory capture's third face of power. *Socio-Economic Review*, 21(2), 1217–45.

Lieberman, E.S. 2005. Nested analysis as a mixed-method strategy for comparative research. *American Political Science Review*, 99(3), 435–52.

Lindblom, C.E. 1959. The science of 'muddling through'. *Public Administration Review*, 19(2), 79–88.

Lippmann, W. 1965. *Public Opinion*. The Free Press.

Locke, J. 1996 [1689]. *An Essay Concerning Human Understanding* II.i, edited by K.P. Winkler. Hackett Publishing Company.

Lopez, B. 2020. Love in a time of terror: On natural landscapes, metaphorical living, and Warlpiri identity. *Literary Hub*, 7, 2020. Available at: https://lithub.com/barry-lopez-love-in-a-time-of-terror/ [Accessed 19 July 2024].

Lord, C. 2013. *Aristotle's politics*. University of Chicago Press.

Lupton, D. 2016. *The Quantified Self*. Polity.

Lyon, D. 2014. Surveillance, Snowden, and big data: Capacities, consequences, critique. *Big Data and Society*, 1(2), pp 1–13.

Mann, S. 2009. Sousveillance: Wearable computing and citizen 'undersight' – watching from below rather than above. *h+ Magazine*, 10 July. Available at: https://www.hplusmagazine.com/2009/07/sousveillance-wearable-computing-and-citizen-undersight-watching-from-below-rather-than-above/ [Accessed 10 September 2024].

Marcuse, H. 1964. *One Dimensional Man*. Beacon Press.

Marichal, J. 2012. *Facebook Democracy: The Architecture of Disclosure and the Threat to Public Life*. Taylor & Francis.

Marshall, T.H. 1964. *Class, Citizenship, and Social Development*. Doubleday.

Martel, J.R. 2017. *The Misinterpellated Subject*. Duke University Press.

Marwick, A. and Lewis, R. 2017. *Media Manipulation and Disinformation Online*. Data & Society Research Institute.

Masinsin, M. 2025. Data localization: A global threat to human rights online. *Freedom House*, 8 April. Available at: https://freedomhouse.org/article/data-localization-global-threat-human-rights-online [Accessed 25 January 2025].

Massumi, B. 2015. *Ontopower: War, Powers, and the State of Perception*. Duke University Press.

McKelvey, F. and Neves, J. 2021. Introduction: Optimization and its discontents. *Review of Communication*, 21(2), pp 95–112.

Mehl, M.R., Vazire, S., Ramírez-Esparza, N., Slatcher, R.B. and Pennebaker, J.W. 2007. Are women really more talkative than men?. *Science*, 317(5834), 82.

Meltwater. 2025. Digital 2025 April Global Statshot Report. *DataReportal*. Available at: https://datareportal.com/reports/digital-2025-april-global-statshot [Accessed 23 April 2025].

Merton, R.K. and Barber, E. 2004. *The Travels and Adventures of Serendipity: A Study in Sociological Semantics and the Sociology of Science*. Princeton University Press.

Mill, J.S. 2002 [1859]. *On Liberty, The Basic Writings of John Stuart Mill*. The Modern Library.

Mises, L.V. 1963. *Human Action: A Treatise on Economics*. 3rd rev. ed. Henry Regnery.

Mora, G.C. 2014. *Making Hispanics: How Activists, Bureaucrats, and Media Constructed a New American*. University of Chicago Press.

Morozov, E. 2014. Making it: Pick up a spot welder and join the revolution. *The New Yorker*, 13 January. Available at: https://www.newyorker.com/magazine/2014/01/13/making-it-2 [Accessed 20 August 2024].

Morning Consult. 2023. Influencer marketing trends report. *Morning Consult*. Available at: https://pro.morningconsult.com/analyst-reports/influencer-marketing-trends-report [Accessed 21 June 2024].

Morris, J.W., Prey, R. and Nieborg, D. B. 2021. Engineering culture: Logics of optimization in music, games, and apps. *Review of Communication*, 21(2), 161–75.

Mouffe, C. 2005. *The Return of the Political*. Verso.

Murphy Kelly, S. 2022. Their teenage children died by suicide. Now these families want to hold social media companies accountable. *CNN Business*, 19 April. Available at: https://www.cnn.com/2022/04/19/tech/social-media-lawsuits-teen-suicide/index.html [Accessed 27 January 2025].

N+1 Editors 2023. Why is everything so ugly? *n+1*, 44. Available at: https://www.nplusonemag.com/issue-44/the-intellectual-situation/why-is-everything-so-ugly/ [Accessed 15 July 2024].

Nedelsky, J. 1989. Reconceiving autonomy: Sources, thoughts and possibilities. *Yale Journal of Law & Feminism*, 1, 7–36.

Negri, A. 1999. *Insurgencies: Constituent Power and the Modern State.* University of Minnesota Press.

Nozick, R. 1974. *Anarchy, State, and Utopia.* Blackwell.

Online Safety Act 2023, c. 50. Available at: https://www.legislation.gov.uk/ukpga/2023/50/contents/enacted [Accessed 25 February 2025].

Olma, S. 2016. *In Defence of Serendipity.* Duncan Baird Publishers.

Ortutay, B. 2024. What to know about the Kids Online Safety Act that just passed the Senate. *AP News,* 31 July. Available at: https://apnews.com/article/congress-social-media-kosa-kids-online-safety-act-parents-ead646422cf84cef0d0573c3c841eb6d [Accessed 25 January 2025].

Pasquale, F. 2015. *The Black Box Society: The Secret Algorithms That Control Money and Information.* Harvard University Press.

Pateman, C. 1975. *Participation and Democratic Theory.* Cambridge University Press.

Peale, N.V. 1952. *The Power of Positive Thinking.* New York: Fawcett Crest.

Pelley, L. 2017. The problem with Muzak. Spotify's bid to remodel an industry. *The Baffler,* 37. Available at: https://thebaffler.com/salvos/the-problem-with-spotify [Accessed 12 September 2024].

Phillips, W. and Milner, R.M. 2017. *The Ambivalent Internet: Mischief, Oddity and Antagonism Online.* Polity Press.

Popper, K.R. 1963. *Conjectures and Refutations: The Growth of Scientific Knowledge.* Routledge and Kegan Paul.

Power, E. 2022. Elon Musk is inspired by Iain Banks's utopian sci-fi novels – but he doesn't understand them. *The Telegraph,* 15 November. Available at: https://www.telegraph.co.uk/books/what-to-read/does-elon-musk-really-understand-books-claims-inspired/ [Accessed 12 August 2024].

Ragin, C.C. 2000. *Fuzzy-set Social Science.* University of Chicago Press.

Risse, M. 2021. The fourth generation of human rights: Epistemic rights in digital lifeworlds. *Moral Philosophy and Politics,* 8(2), 351–78.

Risse, M. 2023. *Political Theory of the Digital Age: Where Artificial Intelligence Might Take Us.* Cambridge University Press.

Roth, A. 2024. Microsoft sued by programmers over CodePilot's use of GitHub code. *The Register,* 17 January. Available at: https://www.theregister.com/2024/01/17/microsoft_codepilot_github_lawsuit/ [Accessed 18 September 2024].

Roth, E. 2023. The *New York Times* sues OpenAI for copyright infringement. *The Verge,* 27 December. Available at: https://www.theverge.com/2023/12/27/24016212/new-york-times-openai-microsoft-lawsuit-copyright-infringement [Accessed 7 September 2024].

Rothbard, M.N. 1998 [1982]. *The Ethics of Liberty.* New York University Press.

Samuel, S. 2024. Black Nazis? A woman pope? That's just the start of Google's AI problem. *Vox,* 28 February. Available at: https://www.vox.com/future-perfect/2024/2/28/24083814/google-gemini-ai-bias-ethics [Accessed 4 September 2024].

Rousseau, J.-J. 1920. *The Social Contract & Discourses*. Project Gutenberg. Available at: http://www.gutenberg.org/ebooks/46333 [Accessed 30 January 2025].

Sandel, M.J. 1988. The political theory of the procedural republic. *Revue de Métaphysique et de Morale*, 93(1), 57–68.

Sartre, J.P. 2007. *Existentialism is a Humanism*. Yale University Press.

Schattschneider, E.E. 1960. *The Semisovereign People: A Realist's View of Democracy in America*. Holt, Rinehart and Winston.

Schmitt, C. 2007. *The Concept of the Political: Expanded Edition*. Translated by G. Schwab, with an introduction by T.B. Strong and a foreword by L. Strauss. University of Chicago Press

Scott, J.C. 1998. *Seeing Like a State: How Certain Schemes to Improve the Human Condition Have Failed*. Yale University Press.

Searle, J. 1980. Minds, brains and programs. *Behavioral and Brain Sciences*, 3, 417–57.

Shannon, C.E. 1948. A mathematical theory of communication. *The Bell System Technical Journal*, 27(3), 379–423.

Shariatmadari, D. 2023. 'I hope I'm wrong': The co-founder of DeepMind on how AI threatens to reshape life as we know it. *The Guardian*, 2 September. Available at: https://www.theguardian.com/books/2023/sep/02/i-hope-im-wrong-the-co-founder-of-deepmind-on-how-ai-threatens-to-reshape-life-as-we-know-it [Accessed 15 September 2024].

Shehu, A. and Shehu, S. 2003. Human rights in the technology era – protection of data rights. *European Journal of Economics, Law and Social Sciences*, 7(2), 6–15.

Shorten, R. 2021. *The Ideology of Political Reactionaries*. Routledge.

Siegel, L. 2022. *Why Argument Matters*. Yale University Press.

Simon, H.A. 1987. 'Satisficing'. In *Models of Bounded Rationality, Volume 3: Empirically Grounded Economic Reason*. The MIT Press, pp 295–8.

Simon, H.A. 2000. Bounded rationality in social science: Today and tomorrow. *Mind & Society*, 1(1), 25–39.

Simons, J. 2023. *Algorithms for the People: Democracy in the Age of AI*. Princeton University Press.

Singh, M. and Singh, J. 2022. India sets up panel with veto power over social media content moderation. *TechCrunch*, 28 October. Available at: https://techcrunch.com/2022/10/28/india-to-create-committees-with-veto-power-over-social-media-content-moderation/ [Accessed 25 January 2025].

Smith, A. 2010 [1759]. *The Theory of Moral Sentiments*. Penguin.

Splitter, J. 2021. The way we eat could lead to habitat loss for 17,000 species by 2050. *Vox*, 18 February. Available at: https://www.vox.com/future-perfect/22287498/meat-wildlife-biodiversity-species-plantbased [Accessed 10 September 2024].

Srinivasan, D. 2020. Why Google dominates advertising markets. *Stanford Technology Law Review*, 24(1), 55–175.

Srnicek, N. 2017. *Platform Capitalism*. Polity.

St. Aubin, C. and Liedke, J. 2024a. News Platform Fact Sheet. Pew Research Center, 29 October. Available at: https://www.pewresearch.org/journalism/fact-sheet/news-platform-fact-sheet/ [Accessed 13 October 2024].

St. Aubin, C. and Liedke, J. 2024b. Social Media and News Fact Sheet. Pew Research Center, 29 October. Available at: https://www.pewresearch.org/journalism/fact-sheet/social-media-and-news-fact-sheet/ [Accessed 20 October 2024].

Stone, D. 1988. *Policy Paradox: The Art of Political Decision Making*. W.W. Norton & Co.

Suleyman, M. 2023. *The Coming Wave: Technology, Power, and the Twenty-First Century's Greatest Dilemma*. Crown.

Sumpter, D.J.T. 2018. *Outnumbered: From Facebook and Google to Fake News and Filter-Bubbles – The Algorithms That Control Our Lives*. Bloomsbury.

Taleb, N.N. 2010. *The Black Swan: The Impact of the Highly Improbable*. Random House.

Tau, B. 2024. *Means of Control: How the Hidden Alliance of Tech and Government Is Creating a New American Surveillance State*. Crown.

Taylor, C. 1994. 'The Politics of Recognition'. In A. Gutmann (ed) *Multiculturalism and the Politics of Recognition*. Princeton University Press, pp 25–73.

Taylor, C. 2007. *A Secular Age*. Harvard University Press.

Technical.ly 2024. Tech lobbying spending surged in 2023, report finds. Available at: https://www.technical.ly/2024/01/tech-lobbying-spending-2023/ [Accessed 30 October 2024].

Thaler, R.H. and Sunstein, C.R. 2008. *Nudge: Improving Decisions About Health, Wealth, and Happiness*. Yale University Press.

Thatcher, M. 1987. Interview for 'Woman's Own' ('No Such Thing as Society'), in *Margaret Thatcher Foundation: Speeches, Interviews and Other Statements*.

Tocqueville, A. 2006 [1835]. *Democracy in America*. Translated by Henry Reeve. *Project Gutenberg*. Available at: www.gutenberg.org/files/815/815-h/815-h.htm [Accessed 29 March 2025].

Toonders, J. 2014. Data is the new oil of the digital economy. *Wired*. Available at: http://www.wired.com/insights/2014/07/data-new-oil-digital-economy/ [Accessed 30 October 2024].

Trillò, T., Scharlach, R., Hallinan, B., Kim, B., Mizoroki, S., Frosh, P. and Shifman, L. 2021. What does #freedom look like? Instagram and the visual imagination of values. *Journal of Communication*, 71(6), 875–97.

Trist, E.L. 1981. The evolution of socio-technical systems: A conceptual framework and an action research program. *Ontario Quality of Working Life Center*, Occasional Paper no. 2.

Trottier, D. and Fuchs, C. 2014. Theorising social media, politics and the state: An introduction. In D. Trottier and C. Fuchs (eds) *Social Media, Politics and the State: Protests, Revolutions, Riots, Crime and Policing in the Age of Facebook, Twitter and YouTube*. Routledge, pp 3–38.

REFERENCES

Truman, D. 1951. *The Governmental Process: Political Interests and Public Opinion*. Alfred A. Knopf.

Turner, F. 2013. *The Democratic Surround: Multimedia and American Liberalism from World War II to the Psychedelic Sixties*. University of Chicago Press.

Urbina, F., Lentzos, F., Invernizzi, C. and Elkins, S. 2022. Dual use of artificial-intelligence powered drug discovery. *Nature Machine Intelligence*, 4, 189–91.

Vallor, S. 2016. *Technology and the Virtues: A Philosophical Guide to a Future Worth Wanting*. Oxford University Press.

Varoufakis, Y. 2023. *Technofeudalism: What Killed Capitalism*. Melville House.

Veblen, T. 1899. *The Theory of the Leisure Class: An Economic Study of Institutions*. Macmillan.

Vermeule, A. 2020. Rules, commands, and principles in the administrative state. *Yale Law Journal Forum*, 130, pp 356–69.

Vincent, J. 2023. AI art tools Stable Diffusion and Midjourney targeted with copyright lawsuit. *The Verge*, 16 January. Available at: https://www.theverge.com/2023/1/16/23559244/ai-art-tools-stable-diffusion-midjourney-copyright-lawsuit [Accessed 10 September 2024].

Vinsel, L. 2021. You're doing it wrong: Notes on criticism and technology Hype. *Medium*, 1 February. Available at: https://sts-news.medium.com/youre-doing-it-wrong-notes-on-criticism-and-technology-hype-18b08b4307e5 [Accessed 10 September 2024].

Vogell, H. 2022. Rent going up? One company's algorithm could be why. *ProPublica*, 15 October. Available at: https://www.propublica.org/article/yieldstar-rent-increase-realpage-rent [Accessed 10 September 2024].

Vonnegut, K. 1998. *Cat's Cradle: A Novel* (Vol. 1149). Dial Press Trade Paperback.

Vosoughi, S., Roy, D. and Aral, S. 2018. The spread of true and false news online. *Science*, 359(6380), 1146–51.

Wansink, B. 2011. *Mindless Eating*. Hay House UK Limited.

Warren, A. and Mavroudi, E. 2011. Managing surveillance? The impact of biometric residence permits on UK migrants. *Journal of Ethnic and Migration Studies*, 37(9), 1495–1511.

Warren, S.D. and Brandeis, L.D. 1890. The right to privacy. *Harvard Law Review*, 4(5), 193–220.

Weber, M. 1946. Science as a vocation. In A. Tauber (ed) *Science and the Quest for Reality*. Palgrave Macmillan UK, pp 382–94.

Weber, L. and Malhi, S. 2024. Women are getting off birth control amid misinformation explosion. *The Washington Post*, 21 March. Available at: https://www.washingtonpost.com/health/2024/03/21/stopping-birth-control-misinformation/ [Accessed 6 September 2024].

Weil, S. 2023. *Simone Weil: Basic Writings*. Taylor & Francis.

Whitney, D. 2022. Diego Rivera's resolute socialism is on full display in his mural *Pan American Unity*. *Jacobin*, 25 October. Available at: https://jacobin.com/2022/10/diego-rivera-socialist-art-pan-american-unity-mural [Accessed 10 September 2024].

Whitman, W. 1855. Leaves of grass. Available at: https://www.whitmanarchive.org [Accessed 10 September 2024].

Wilde, O. 1923. *The Decay of Lying* (Vol. 5). Doubleday, Page.

Wilhelm, H. and Kellner, T. 2022. Amazon is making your life easier through ambient intelligence. *Amazon*, 5 October. Available at: https://www.aboutamazon.com/news/devices/amazon-is-making-your-life-easier-through-ambient-intelligence [Accessed 15 September 2024].

Wilkinson, P. 2010. *International Relations*. Sterling Publishing Company.

Winner, L. 1980. Do artifacts have politics? *Daedalus*, 109(1), 121–36.

Winthrop, J. 1630. *A Model of Christian Charity*. Project Gutenberg. Available at: www.gutenberg.org/ebooks/66701 [Accessed 29 April 2025].

Wolin, S.S. 1994. Fugitive democracy. *Constellations: An International Journal of Critical & Democratic Theory*, 1(1), 11–25.

Woo, G. 2002. Quantitative terrorism risk assessment. *The Journal of Risk Finance*, 4(1), 7–14.

Woods, D. 2022. I'm a former CIA cyber-operations officer who studies bot traffic. Here's why it's plausible that more than 80% of Twitter's accounts are actually fake – and Twitter is not alone. *F5*, 14 July. Available at: https://www.f5.com/company/blog/bot-traffic-percentage-fake-accounts-expert [Accessed 11 September 2024].

Wu, T. 2011. *The Master Switch: The Rise and Fall of Information Empires*. Vintage.

Wulf, A. 2022. *Magnificent Rebels: The First Romantics and the Invention of the Self*. Vintage.

YouTube. 2025. Culture & trends report 2025: Virtual creators. *YouTube*. Available at: https://www.youtube.com/trends/report/tr25-virtual-creators/ [Accessed 28 March 2025].

Zuboff, S. 2019. *The Age of Surveillance Capitalism: The Fight for a Human Future at the New Frontier of Power*. Public Affairs.

Zuckerberg, M. 2017. Mark Zuckerberg delivers keynote address at Facebook's F8 Developer Conference. *Youtube*. Available at: https://www.youtube.com/watch?v=mKYpm3OFcvY [Accessed 13 May 2025].

Zuckerman, E. 2014. The Internet's original sin. *The Atlantic*, 14 August. Available at: https://www.theatlantic.com/technology/archive/2014/08/advertising-is-the-internets-original-sin/376041/ [Accessed 10 September 2024].

Index

A

abstraction 1, 9, 15, 17, 52, 56, 96, 98
AI (artificial intelligence)
 alignment problem 15
 generative 16, 103, 111
 and potentiality 114–15
Airoldi, M. 7, 93, 105
algorithmic contract 1–10
 and anxiety 3, 8, 43–4, 46
 and autonomy 7, 12, 44
 and classification 1, 7, 12, 17, 51–2
 and desire 9, 71–2
 renegotiation of i, 10, 105, 121–2
algorithmic problem i, 5, 7, 14, 61, 84, 122
Althusser, Louis 114
Amazon 9, 67, 71, 74, 82
Amoore, L. 115, 116, 121
Arendt, Hannah 23, 56, 99, 100, 101
Aristotle 17, 34, 35, 111
authoritarianism 17, 23, 83, 100
autonomy 2, 7, 12, 44, 61, 81, 105, 109, 122

B

Bail, Chris 39, 56
Banks, Iain 83
Bataille, George 88
Baudrillard, Jean 33
Beer, D. 10, 87, 106
Benjamin, Walter 46
Berlin, Isaiah 37
Bernays, Edward 77
Bonini, T. and Trere, E. 10, 120, 121
Borges, Jorge Luis 43
Brandeis, Louis 20, 122
Brubaker, R. 40

C

Cambridge Analytica 11–13, 74, 107
Chappell, S.G. 115
Chayka, Kyle 33, 122
Cheney-Lippold, J. 21, 22
choice 2, 8, 43–45, 52

classification 1
 algorithmic 3, 7, 52–5
 and identity 21, 46, 48
 and politics 68, 69
commodification 4, 8, 47, 71, 78, 100
Crawford, Kate 24, 25
Crockett, M.J. 41

D

Dahl, Robert 61
Deleuze, Gilles 22
Deneen, Patrick 35
desire 9, 71, 72, 78
Dick, Phillip K. 1
Dorsey, Jack 39, 105
Durkheim, Émile 45

E

Eco, Umberto 88
Emerson, Ralph Waldo 9, 85, 86, 90, 94
epistemic rights 10, 108–9, 111
extraordinary politics 10, 119–21

F

Facebook 11, 13, 42, 47, 49, 78, 87
factory farming 18, 96, 101–4
Feyerabend, Paul 112
Fish, Adam 9, 77, 107
Fisher, Eran 8, 17, 43, 44, 45
Flisfeder, Matthew 9, 71, 72, 73
Fogg, B.J. 91
Foucault, Michel 13, 21, 56, 97
Fourcade, Marion 8, 20, 47, 50
Frank, Jason 119
Fricker, Miranda 108
frontier 9, 75, 90

G

Giddens, Anthony 55
Gilliard, C. 80, 82
Gioia, Ted 31, 32
Gladwell, Malcolm 18
Google 47, 71, 74, 107, 114
Grove, J. 59

H

Han, Byung-Chul 10, 96, 97, 99
Harris, Tristan 91
Hayek, Friedrich 66, 69
Healy, Kieran 8, 20, 47, 50
Heidegger, Martin 92, 93
Hobbes, Thomas 3, 17, 36, 40, 41
Hong, S. 89

I

identity
  algorithmic 21, 22, 55, 98
  optimization of 85–104
Igo, Sarah 19, 20
inviolate personality 20, 122
isolation 9, 40, 98, 99

J

Jobs, Steve 95

K

Kafka, Franz 55, 68
Kalyvas, Andreas 10, 119, 120
Kant, Immanuel 14, 37, 44, 45, 108
Khan, Lina 70
Kierkegaard, Søren 96
kipple 1, 2, 62
Kogan, Aleksandr 11
Kurzweil, Ray 86

L

Labatut, B. 94
Lacan, Jacques 72, 73
Lanier, Jaron 76
Larkin, Daniel 106
Lefebvre, Henri 109, 115
liberalism
  neoliberalism 9, 65, 71, 96, 106, 109
  technoliberalism 9, 77, 87, 107, 114
Lippmann, Walter 105
local minima 6, 7, 28, 55, 90, 97, 101, 106, 122
Locke, John 3, 17, 37, 51, 52
Lupton, Deborah 81
Lyon, David 36

M

Marcuse, Herbert 78, 100
Martel, James 114, 115
Massumi, Brian 56, 57
Mill, John Stuart 44, 63
Mouffe, Chantal 61, 64
Musk, Elon 38, 53, 83, 95

N

Negri, Antonio 120
Nix, Alexander 11
Nozick, Robert 83

O

OpenAI 16, 18, 38, 70, 108
optimization 1, 19
  of democracy 34–42
  and politics of 8, 24–33
ordinal society 8, 46, 47, 51, 94
outliers 2, 5, 18, 61, 81, 83

P

Pasquale, Frank 15, 50, 69
Peale, Norman Vincent 95
Pelley, L. 31
pi.fyi (platform) 10, 122
Popper, Karl 63
potentiality 10, 109, 114–16, 121
power 13, 21, 52, 56, 60
pre-emption 57–9
prediction 1, 2, 6, 13, 14, 15, 88
privacy 2, 19, 20

R

Ragin, C.C. 117
Rand, Ayn 62
Ring cameras 4, 9, 80, 81
Risse, Mathias 10, 108, 109, 111
Rivera, Diego 24
Róna, Jaroslav 55
Rousseau, Jean-Jacques 3

S

Sandel, Michael 34
Sartre, Jean-Paul 43, 44, 46
Schattschneider, E.E. 53
Schmitt, Carl 98
Scott, James 19, 20, 22, 23
Searle, John 103
serendipity 7, 10, 109, 110–14
Simon, H.A. 67
Simons, J. 61
Smith, Adam 48
social contract 3, 17, 46, 50, 52
Srinivasan, Balaji 62
Srnicek, N. 73
surveillance 9
  capitalism 75
  luxury 9, 80, 81

T

Taleb, Nassim 88, 89
Tau, Byron 12, 74
Taylor, Charles 16, 83
Thatcher, Margaret 66
Thiel, Peter 62
Thoreau, Henry David 9, 87
Tocqueville, Alexis de 86
totalitarianism 23, 65, 99, 100
Truman, David 61
Turner, Fred 9, 87, 90

INDEX

V

Vallor, Shannon 34
Veblen, T. 78
Vonnegut, Kurt 117

W

Warren, Samuel 20, 122
Weber, Max 14
Weil, Simone 97
Whitman, Walt 9, 55, 85, 96
Wilde, Oscar 116, 117
Winner, L. 24
Winthrop, John 90
Wolin, Sheldon 120
Wulf, Andrea 98

X

X (formerly Twitter) 5, 38, 40, 42

Z

Zuboff, Shoshana 13, 47, 75
Zuckerberg, Mark 38, 48, 53, 86
Zuckerman, Ethan 75, 76

www.ingramcontent.com/pod-product-compliance
Lightning Source LLC
Chambersburg PA
CBHW071715020426
42333CB00017B/2283